Praise for

Find Your Miracle

"Kerry and Chris Shook present an amazing view on miracles and how we experience them today. In showing us fresh ways to look at Scripture, they encourage us that the miracles Christ did while on earth have relevance for us today. Reading this book will inspire you with a new sense of faith!"

—MATTHEW BARNETT, CEO of The Dream Center, Los Angeles, CA

"As Chris and Kerry unpack the miracles of Jesus, they show us that miracles are not the focus. They are just the road signs pointing to God—to a real and personal relationship with Him."

—MARK BATTERSON, lead pastor of National Community Church, Washington, DC, and *New York Times* best-selling author of *The Circle Maker*

"Let's face it. At times we all need a miracle. Whether you are overwhelmed, feeling alone, or afraid, God is able to meet your needs. Every single one of them. Kerry and Chris Shook have written a powerful book based on Jesus's intervention in the lives of people in need of a miracle. I encourage you to apply the principles in *Find Your Miracle* and watch God impact your life like never before!"

—DR. JACK GRAHAM, pastor of Prestonwood Baptist Church, Dallas, TX, and author of *Angels*

"Many of us feel lonely, overwhelmed, and afraid and long for relief. At some point everyone needs a miracle. In their powerful new book *Find Your Miracle*, Kerry and Chris Shook show us how the miracles of Jesus can grow our faith, strengthen our resolve, and deepen our relationship with the Miracle Maker."

—CRAIG GROESCHEL, pastor of Life.Church, Oklahoma City, and author of *#Struggles: Following Jesus in a Selfie-Centered World*

"Wow! Kerry and Chris Shook have blessed us again with a fantastic biblical feast in *Find Your Miracle*. I loved the depth of studying many of Jesus's miracles without losing the practical application of how my life is impacted every day by God's supernatural provision. This book reminds us that God turns our messes into messages, our pain into purpose, and our greatest barriers into bridges of healing and ministry. I encourage you to take this wonderful journey through the miracles of Jesus and be prepared to experience your own blessing as you search for the miracles God has for you."

—ALAN ROBERTSON, star of A&E's *Duck Dynasty* and coauthor of
A New Season and *The Duck Commander Devotional for Couples*

"God is still in the miracle business! Let the long-ago miraculous acts of Jesus guide you into understanding how God can intervene in your life today. Whether you're overwhelmed, discouraged, hurting, or afraid, my friends Kerry and Chris Shook will draw you a map to your miracle."

—LEE STROBEL, best-selling author of *The Case for Christ*
and *The Case for Grace*

"God is personal and present today. Chris and Kerry Shook unpack the miracles of Jesus in *Find Your Miracle* and remind us of this earth-shattering, faith-building, miracle-expecting truth that makes all the difference in our lives right now."

—ROMA DOWNEY, producer and actress

"With great clarity and insight, the Shooks show us that experiencing the miracles of God requires more participation on our part than what we may initially expect. Read with caution—this book will push you past your comfort zone as you're delivered to the other side of your doubts."

—STEVEN FURTICK, pastor of Elevation Church, Charlotte, NC,
and *New York Times* best-selling author of *(Un)Qualified*

FIND
YOUR
MIRACLE

FIND YOUR MIRACLE

HOW THE MIRACLES OF JESUS CAN CHANGE YOUR LIFE TODAY

KERRY & CHRIS
SHOOK

WATERBROOK

We dedicate this book to our amazing children and grandchildren—
Steven, Jordan, Megan, Josh, Kelli, Ryan, Sarah, Ben, and Joanna—
for all your encouragement. You are true miracles of God.

Contents

JESUS: THE LIFE GIVER

A Note to the Reader

Even though we are two different people with different personalities and perspectives, we always write our books in first person. We find this avoids the cumbersome task of constantly inserting "Kerry" or "Chris" before each paragraph, section, or chapter. More important, however, as husband and wife, we believe we are one person in spirit, and we want to communicate our heartfelt message to you as one voice from one heart. We have found that God uses us more effectively when we communicate as a husband-and-wife team.

Jesus: The Source of Miracles

Don't seek miracles. Follow Jesus. And if you follow Jesus
long enough and far enough, you'll eventually find yourself
in the middle of some miracles.

—Mark Batterson

Jesus' miracles are not just a challenge to our minds, but a
promise to our hearts, that the world we all want is coming.

—Timothy Keller

1

The Miracle You Need Most

I never have any difficulty believing in miracles since I
experienced the miracle of a change in my own heart.

—Augustine

"What do you want me to do for you?" Jesus asked him.
The blind man said, "Rabbi, I want to see."

—Mark 10:51

I BELIEVE IN MIRACLES.

I believe in the miracles of the Bible, the miracles of Jesus, and, yes, I believe
that miracles happen today.

I believe miracles are not just natural occurrences that seem amazing yet
have scientific explanations. I believe miracles are, in fact, instances of God en-
tering into His creation, the natural order, to do supernatural things.

And I believe that God's transformation of a human heart, His hand reaching into a person's daily existence and turning a life around, is the greatest miracle anyone can experience. It's a supernatural act called redemption.

So, yes, I believe in miracles.

But I realize many disagree with me. They say, "How can you possibly believe in miracles in our modern scientific age?"

Well, these modern times reflect some interesting and surprising things about people's attitudes toward miracles.

Today a startling number of people who label themselves Christians don't believe in supernatural miracles, while many so-called secular people do. Today a new generation of atheists tries to debunk the reality of miracles even as science seems to uncover phenomena that point to a Power beyond. Today many people consider a belief in miracles embarrassing even as those same people deeply long for them.

We seem to have an attraction to the possibility of miracles at the same time we are skeptical about them.

Some pastors, theologians, and churches explain away the miracles of the Bible and dismiss the reality of miracles today. One New Testament professor wrote, "Despite the prominence of miracles in the Gospel traditions, I don't think historians can show that any of them, including the resurrection, ever happened."[1] A former bishop in the Episcopal Church has written that the miracles in the Bible cannot "be interpreted . . . as supernatural events."[2] A contemporary theologian said, "Because I do not accept this way of thinking about the world and God's relation to the world, I avoid the term 'miracles.'"[3]

These voices are a part of the church that claims the name "Christian" yet tries to rewrite Christianity to exclude the supernatural and deny the existence of miracles, both in biblical times and now. They say what the Bible calls miracles were merely events that amazed people because they were ignorant of the rules of nature and the principles of science. These people preach a different gospel, which isn't the gospel at all.

This part of the church is literally dying. It's taken the "beyond" out of the gospel. It's taken the deity out of Jesus. It's taken the supernatural out of miracles. It is left with a faith that doesn't require faith. No wonder its numbers are dwindling. Many people long for what this church has chosen to deny.

It's a common misperception that most people in America do not believe in miracles. In fact, 79 percent of Americans say they believe miracles happen. You might think the percentage of young people—Millennials—who believe in miracles would drop substantially. Yes, it does drop but by just one point—to 78 percent.[4] People of all ages still believe in miracles. Most of us, regardless of our age, have this inner sense that there must be something more than we can see.

These longings point to the message of the gospel.

The true gospel says we are not merely physical beings but spiritual beings as well. The true gospel reveals a God who fashioned nature and stands above it, a God who is super-nature. The true gospel shows God reaching into our natural world and doing supernatural things. The true gospel reports how Jesus, the Son of God, entered our broken, natural world and walked among us, fully human and fully divine.

THE REAL STEP OF FAITH

C. S. Lewis talked about some belief systems that acknowledge the presence of God but claim He is distant and apart. Lewis called this by the general term *pantheism,* but for him it also covered what some might call belief in a spiritual power or deism or Modernism.[5]

In order to believe in miracles, you and I need to believe that God enters into the natural world and acts specifically in a particular life. We need to accept that He's not just a spiritual power or a universal force or a distant deity but is, in fact, personal and present in our lives today.

To me, this is the real step of faith. Believing there is something more than nature, something beyond science, is the easy part. The hard part is to believe God is personal. So personal that He breaks through the natural order in various ways to make Himself known, to accomplish something supernatural, and, yes, to save us from ourselves.

True Christian faith claims that God became personal. God, who was outside the system, entered into the system Himself. Jesus, who is God in human form, entered creation at a specific moment in time.

Believing this is the real step of faith.

As we look at the miracles of Jesus, we need to remember that this was also a real step of faith for the people who encountered Him in those places and at that time. The wedding guests, the sick and the paralyzed, the crowds who heard Him teach, the fishermen on the Sea of Galilee, the Pharisees who resented Him, the thousands on a hillside who suddenly were supplied with food—each and every one of them had to face these questions: *Who is this Jesus? Was this really a miracle? Is this Jesus actually God? And if He is, does that mean God is really here with us?*

It is good for us today to step into their shoes because their questions are our questions. For the Jews, who had lived for hundreds of years under a system of law and sacrifices, could they accept this Jesus was Yahweh in person? Could He be the long-awaited Messiah? For Romans and Greeks, who believed in a pantheon of gods and various myths about how they lived in the heavens, was it possible that Jesus was actually the one and only God, walking on earth? For Samaritans and fishermen and others outside the religious and political systems, who was this remarkable Healer? Possibly God Himself?

One particular person, a fisherman, was with Jesus from the beginning of His ministry on earth. This fisherman was at the center of many of the events and was a witness to many of the miracles in Jesus's life. It's interesting to me that only after many experiences with Jesus, spanning perhaps most of three years, finally Simon Peter became a true believer:

[Jesus] asked his disciples, "Who do people say the Son of Man is?"

They replied, "Some say John the Baptist; others say Elijah; and still others, Jeremiah or one of the prophets."

"But what about you?" he asked. "Who do you say I am?"

Simon Peter answered, "You are the Messiah, the Son of the living God." (Matthew 16:13–16)

Believing that Jesus was a prophet or a magician or a good man or a captivating teacher was easy. Believing that Jesus was the Son of God was the real step of faith.

That's still true for us today. Through His miracles, one after another, Jesus asks you and me this question: "Who do you say I am?" When John the Baptist sent his followers to inquire of Jesus if He was a prophet or the Messiah, Jesus replied, "Go back and report to John what you hear and see: The blind receive sight, the lame walk, those who have leprosy are cleansed, the deaf hear, the dead are raised, and the good news is proclaimed to the poor" (Matthew 11:4–5). Jesus was saying, "If you need help with the real step of faith, look at the miracles I do."

You see, the miracles of Jesus have much to say about Jesus. They have much to say about you and me. And they consistently raise the question that exists in between: "Who do you say I am?"

GOD STILL WORKS MIRACLES

Tiffany Gilliam received a call from her husband, Shane. Their son, Braedyn, had been in an accident and was in serious condition. Tiffany prayed as she rushed to the hospital. Braedyn remained in the hospital for two more weeks, but he made an inexplicable recovery. Tiffany and Shane now call Braedyn their "miracle boy."[6]

Many people say that the miracles of the Bible were real but that miracles no longer happen today. They say that it was a different era, that God doesn't work miracles in this era. They say that what happened to Braedyn was not really a miracle.

I disagree.

The Bible is clear that after Jesus ascended into heaven, the apostles and leaders of the early church performed miracles by the power of the Holy Spirit and in the name of Jesus. Church history is full of accounts of miracles. And today, in this age of science and technology, we hear about remarkable events, such as the story of Braedyn, events that seem impossible and yet actually occurred.

Since the gospel is the story of God, who came to be among us, to be present and personal, then it is as true today as it was two thousand years ago. "God is with us" is the message of miracles, and He is present in our lives right now. So, yes, I believe miracles happen, still, today.

MORE THAN A MIRACLE

But there are dangers in how some people approach miracles today.

Some people see a miracle around every corner; they claim a miracle in almost every situation in life. But not every unusual occurrence is a miracle; some are just natural circumstances. And some things labeled as miracles are trivial. To say it was a miracle when the underdog team won the World Series or when the watch you lost last spring was suddenly found in the corner of the garage indicates a misunderstanding of what true miracles are. In life we encounter many remarkable events, close calls, and near misses that, in the emotion of the moment, we call miracles. Yet they may just be occurrences within the natural order, not evidence of supernatural intervention.

I do believe God wants us to pray about the little things that bother us, because He cares about every detail of our lives. Just this week I lost my debit card after I had used it at the grocery store. When I got home and couldn't find it in my wallet or my car, I drove back to the store. I thought maybe I had dropped it in the parking lot when I took my keys out of my pocket. After searching the parking lot and coming up empty, I started to get really frustrated thinking about all the trouble of canceling my card and getting a new one. I picked up my cell phone to make the call to start the long, drawn-out process, and then it hit me. *I haven't even prayed about it! I'm frustrated. I'm angry. But I haven't whispered a single sentence of a prayer!*

So I stopped and just said, "God, please show me where my debit card is, and forgive me for not praying sooner." At the exact moment I finished praying, my cell phone slipped out of my hand and fell between the two front seats. I reached down to get it, and the first thing my hand touched was a plastic card. Yes, it was my debit card! I'm still looking for my cell phone, however!

No. I found them both, and I just smiled and thought, *God, You must have a great sense of humor, and I still have so much to learn about trusting You with the details of my life.*

Was finding my debit card a miracle? Not really. But it *was* an answer to prayer. When God helps us in the details of life, maybe we can call those times minor miracles, but we have to be careful describing them as miracles. The problem, of course, is that we dilute the significance of miracles if they aren't rare. And in our ongoing conversation with skeptics, we believers lose the debate. The skeptic says, "You're calling natural things—even trivial things—supernatural."

I also see a danger in making miracles the main focus of our faith. These days, miracles are at the forefront of our culture, right? Collections of miracle stories are published, faith-based healing services are plentiful, and some people even write about and preach miracles as a new gospel, as the object of faith. Now I'm not saying that all faith healing is fakery or that any particular faith healer is a fraud. I think God sometimes works through those people and that approach. But I don't believe God gives miracles just to those who have an abundance of faith and withholds miracles from those who have less faith. That way of thinking only leads to doubt, grief, and disappointment. And that isn't the God I know.

When we exalt miracles as the focus of our belief, we make miracles an idol. Instead, we need to understand that miracles are signs pointing to God and to our need for Him.

So how do we make sense of miracles today? How do we ensure our understanding of miracles in daily life is proper and balanced? How do we properly and fully experience the work that God is doing in our lives through miracles?

A good starting point is to examine the miracles of Jesus. I think we learn much about ourselves and about God by looking at Jesus's miraculous works in the lives of people around Him. I think we can find the miracle we need today through the miracles of Jesus back then. I like what Mark Batterson said: "Don't seek miracles. Follow Jesus."[7]

When you look for your miracle in Jesus, you find more than a miracle. You find Jesus, who is not just the source of miracles. He's the only source of peace, joy, fulfillment, purpose, and meaning.

When my kids were little and I had to travel, I always brought them some small toy or souvenir from wherever I'd been. I would walk in and say, "Daddy's home!" The kids would rush to the door and hug me, and I would open up my suitcase and give them their toys.

They were always excited to get their presents, but they were much more excited about my *presence*. They would pour out all that had happened during the few days I was gone and tell me how they'd missed me so much and were so glad I was home.

The miracles God gives us in this life are the presents, the gifts, that point us to the greater miracle of His presence.

I realize that the miracle you need today may be God's healing touch or God's providing hand. And God can work those miracles in your life, but He'll always do it in a way that will draw you closer to Himself so you can experience the source of the miracle.

Ultimately the biggest danger we face is missing the whole point. Miracles, as we shall see, are not really about physical healing, deliverance from storms, or postponements of a death sentence. Miracles are about God transforming lives spiritually, bringing people into relationship with Him. The point of a miracle is how it brings us closer to God.

So, when it comes to the miracles of Jesus, the end game is Jesus. Christ wants you to find Him and to come into a deep and rich relationship with the God who created you. The ultimate purpose of a miracle is to bring glory to God and draw us closer to Him.

I'm so grateful, however, that Jesus always starts with where we are in order to get us to where we need to be. As we study the miracles of Christ, we see right away that Jesus always met people at their point of need. He got right into their mess so He could give them their miracle.

THE BIG QUESTION

When Jesus was passing through Jericho for the last time on His way to Jerusalem and the cross, He encountered a blind beggar by the name of Bartimaeus. Bartimaeus cried out to Jesus as the crowds pushed in to get a glimpse of the One they had heard worked miracles.

> Jesus stopped and said, "Call him."
>
> So they called to the blind man, "Cheer up! On your feet! He's calling you." Throwing his cloak aside, he jumped to his feet and came to Jesus.
>
> "What do you want me to do for you?" Jesus asked him.
>
> The blind man said, "Rabbi, I want to see." (Mark 10:49–51)

What an interesting question Jesus asked Bartimaeus: "What do you want me to do for you?" Jesus was saying to this blind beggar, "What is the miracle you need most?"

Let's face it. Bartimaeus had lots of needs. He was poor; he needed money. He was probably homeless; he needed a place to live. He was probably alone in life; he needed friends. He could have given Jesus a long list of miracles he needed.

Jesus, however, wanted Bartimaeus to ask for the miracle he needed most. The blind beggar didn't have to think twice. He blurted out, "I want to see." Really, it was a short prayer for a miracle, but it was prayed to the Son of God, the source of miracles.

I believe that is also the starting point for finding your miracle. Jesus asks you, "What is the miracle you need most?" I know it won't take hours or even minutes before the answer comes to your mind. It's the overwhelming burden on your heart right now. Maybe it's so painful you can barely talk about it. The good news is, all you have to do is whisper it to God.

The pathway to a miracle always starts with God asking you, "What is the miracle you need most?" and you telling God and asking Him for your miracle.

Jesus, being all-knowing God, knew how Bartimaeus was going to answer His question. I believe He wanted Bartimaeus to express the miracle he needed most so that he would always remember it was Jesus who answered his short but heartfelt prayer: "I want to see."

As you start the journey to find your miracle, recognize that it always begins with a short and simple prayer. Jesus wants you to clarify the miracle you need most and tell Him in prayer. In Matthew 7:7 Jesus said, "Ask and it will be given to you; seek and you will find; knock and the door will be opened to you."

You will find your miracle only when you seek it by asking the Source of miracles in prayer. Prayer and miracles go hand in hand.

We'll see in the next chapter that Jesus gave Bartimaeus a much greater and longer-lasting miracle than physical sight. Jesus gave him the miracle of a transformed and redeemed life. Jesus started with the miracle Bartimaeus thought he needed most in order to get him what he really needed most—an eternal relationship with the Son of God.

Jesus always starts by asking you the question "What is the miracle you need most?"

As we go on this adventure in faith together, we will end each chapter with powerful, personal promises from God's Word that will encourage you and build your faith in the Source of miracles.

So, what is the miracle you need most? Write it down, and ask Jesus to guide you to your miracle.

Promises for a Miracle

Jesus looked at them and said, "With man this is impossible, but with God all things are possible."

Matthew 19:26

He is the one you praise; he is your God, who performed for you those great and awesome wonders you saw with your own eyes.

Deuteronomy 10:21

I am the LORD, the God of all mankind. Is anything too hard for me?

Jeremiah 32:27

Now glory be to God, who by his mighty power at work within us is able to do far more than we would ever dare to ask or even dream of—infinitely beyond our highest prayers, desires, thoughts, or hopes.

Ephesians 3:20, TLB

He performs wonders that cannot be fathomed,
    miracles that cannot be counted.

Job 5:9

2

The Map to Your Miracle

There are three stages of every great work of God; first it is impossible, then it is difficult, then it is done.

—James Hudson Taylor

When the Sabbath came, he began to teach in the synagogue, and many who heard him were amazed.

"Where did this man get these things?" they asked. "What's this wisdom that has been given him? What are these remarkable miracles he is performing?"

—Mark 6:2

IN GRADE SCHOOL I had to read *Treasure Island,* the Robert Louis Stevenson classic tale of buccaneers and buried gold. Once I began reading, I quickly forgot it was a school assignment. I was completely engrossed in young Jim Hawkins's perilous adventure with pirates that began with the discovery of a treasure map.

The treasure map in Stevenson's novel started the whole fictionalized idea of what a pirate's treasure map is supposed to look like. Because of *Treasure Island,* just about every treasure map in popular culture has an X that marks the spot of the hidden treasure and has dotted lines leading to it.

In the miracles of Christ, I believe we find a real treasure map. It's as if Jesus embedded within the account of each of His miracles a map that can lead us to the X, the spot where we, too, can experience the miracle we need most.

So we need to understand how to read the miracles—how to read the map—because each biblical miracle works on many different levels. It had meaning for people then, but it also has meaning for people now. It revealed something about Jesus then that people clearly responded to, and it reveals something about Jesus to us today. It also becomes a snapshot of people in life situations similar to those in which we find ourselves. Viewed in this way, any one of Jesus's miracles may become the exact miracle you need at a particular time.

Now I'm not saying there's some secret Bible code lurking inside the language of the biblical miracles. And *Find Your Miracle* isn't a magic decoder ring that's the key to a hidden message. But I do believe there are principles that can help you and me find the miracle we need most, one that will bring us into a closer and deeper relationship with the Source of all miracles.

I call these principles the Miracle Map. They are keys to navigating through the miracles, keys to deeper understanding, and keys to applying the truth of Jesus's miracles to our own journeys today. Imagine a traditional map and picture the lower corner. You'll see a legend, a set of color-coded figures that indicate roads, intersections, and significant landmarks.

Likewise, the Miracle Map is a set of pointers that lead to deeper understanding of the miracles and help us navigate our own lives.

THE MIRACLE MAP

There are five principles in the Miracle Map. Not all are present in every miracle that Christ performed, but each miracle has at least one and usually several principles of the Miracle Map.

Let's go into the full story of Bartimaeus and let God open our eyes to the map that can lead us to our miracle.

> Then they came to Jericho. As Jesus and his disciples, together with a large crowd, were leaving the city, a blind man, Bartimaeus (which means "son of Timaeus"), was sitting by the roadside begging. When he heard that it was Jesus of Nazareth, he began to shout, "Jesus, Son of David, have mercy on me!"
>
> Many rebuked him and told him to be quiet, but he shouted all the more, "Son of David, have mercy on me!"
>
> Jesus stopped and said, "Call him."
>
> So they called to the blind man, "Cheer up! On your feet! He's calling you." Throwing his cloak aside, he jumped to his feet and came to Jesus.
>
> "What do you want me to do for you?" Jesus asked him.
>
> The blind man said, "Rabbi, I want to see."
>
> "Go," said Jesus, "your faith has healed you." Immediately he received his sight and followed Jesus along the road. (Mark 10:46–52)

The first principle of the Miracle Map is this: *God always starts with the miracle you need most.* As I said in the first chapter, the journey to find your miracle always begins with God, and God always meets you at the point of your need.

You invite a miracle into your life by bringing your request to Christ, the source of miracles. That's why the Source of miracles asked Bartimaeus, "What do you want me to do for you?" It was the question that prompted the blind beggar to speak his humble and straightforward prayer to Christ: "I want to see."

As you go on this journey to find your miracle, I encourage you to start a prayer journal. A notebook and pen are all you need, or just use your cell phone. Write down the miracle you need most, and then write the date beside it. Every day pray to the source of miracles, Jesus Christ, for your miracle. Every day during your spiritual journey with Jesus, write down what He is teaching you. Don't be afraid to write down your fears, your hurts, your anger and frustration. The psalmist told us to pour out our hearts to God and hold nothing back. One of my favorite verses is 1 Peter 5:7—"[Cast] all your care upon Him, for He cares for you" (NKJV).

It's so comforting to know that the God of the universe cares deeply about my worries, fears, hurts, and needs. Even more comforting is the fact that He has the power to calm my fears, heal my hurts, and meet my needs.

I certainly don't understand the divine mystery of how our prayers and God's miracles come together, but I know God has given us the amazing privilege of bringing our needs, hurts, and burdens to Him in prayer. I also know that God answers prayer!

Jesus asked Bartimaeus the question because He wanted to answer his prayer. Christ asks you the question "What do you want Me to do for you?" or "What is the miracle you need most?" because He wants to answer your prayer.

Jesus told an unusual parable to help His disciples know that they should keep praying and not give up. It was a story about a corrupt and uncaring judge and a helpless widow who came before him and asked him to settle an injustice being done to her by an enemy. At first the judge paid no attention to her just request, but the woman didn't give up. She kept making her request to the judge. Listen to what the judge said in Luke 18:

> The judge ignored her for a while, but finally he said to himself, "I don't fear God or care about people, but this woman is driving me crazy. I'm going to see that she gets justice, because she is wearing me out with her constant requests!" (verses 4–5, NLT)

The judge couldn't care less about the widow, but she bugged him so much that he got sick and tired of her requests. Finally he gave her a favorable ruling so he would never have to deal with her again.

At first glance you might think Jesus was saying that He doesn't really care about answering our prayers but if we constantly bother Him, then He might give in. No. It's just the opposite. Jesus explained the meaning of the parable to His disciples in the next part of the passage.

> Then the Lord said, "Learn a lesson from this unjust judge. Even he rendered a just decision in the end. So don't you think God will surely give justice to his chosen people who cry out to him day and night? Will he keep putting them off?" (verses 6–7, NLT)

I think the point of this parable is not our persistence but God's love. Jesus was saying that if an unjust judge will eventually respond, how much more does God, who loves us, desire to answer our prayers? Jesus was saying we can boldly ask in prayer because we know He loves us so much and wishes to work miracles in our lives.

YOU ARE HERE

When people want me to pray for them, I ask them the same question Jesus asks us: "What is the miracle you need most?"

When someone with cancer asks me to pray, instead of immediately praying for healing, I ask, "How can I pray for you?" Many times they'll say something specific about what they're going through. "Pray for my white blood cell count to go up so I can continue treatment" or "Pray that I get a good report on Tuesday, that the cancer is in remission."

I always pray for God to heal, but I want to follow Christ's example. That's why I ask people what they need. Then I pray for God to meet them first at that point of need.

The Miracle Map is sort of like the map at the mall. It has a big red dot, and next to it are these words: YOU ARE HERE. You can't find your way to where you need to be—in the mall or in life—until you realize where you are.

So where are you right now? I'm not talking about your physical location. I'm talking about where you are on your spiritual journey. Are you close to God? Are you far from God? Are you desperate for a miracle? Do you doubt that God works miracles anymore?

Bartimaeus honestly admitted where he was. In a place of desperation. In a place of great need. In a place of complete darkness. In a place of a deep longing to see!

Jesus always meets us right where we are, but as we'll see in the next principle, He loves us too much to leave us there. He always takes us to where we need to be, so honestly and humbly tell Jesus where you are right now, and ask Him for the miracle you think you need most.

X MARKS THE SPOT

The miracle you need most leads you to what you really need most—a deeper relationship with God. The second principle of the Miracle Map points to relationship.

After Jesus gave Bartimaeus his miracle and he was able to see, Scripture says, "Immediately he received his sight and followed Jesus along the road" (Mark 10:52). I love the imagery of that verse. Bartimaeus physically followed Jesus down the road, but more important, I believe, he followed Jesus with his whole heart and life. That's because miracles never leave us where they find us. Miracles change our path in life or cause us to follow Jesus more closely along that path. Miracles sometimes transport us from a place of being stuck to a place of experiencing freedom. They give us a new, vibrant perspective in place of the old, faded and dim perspective.

Bartimaeus thought the miracle he needed most was healing from his blindness, but what he really needed most was a relationship with Christ, a deep and daily walk with the only source of healing, joy, meaning, peace, and purpose.

That's the X that marks the spot of the real treasure. God starts with the miracle we think we need most, but the real miracle He's trying to take us to is a rich and deep relationship with Him. That is the only treasure that will truly satisfy.

Miracles draw us closer to Christ because they always reveal more of His character. Sometimes when we study the miracles of Christ, we look only at the wow of the miracle, and we miss the wonder of God's character.

In Luke 4:40–41, for example, the Bible speaks of Jesus healing people: "At sunset, the people brought to Jesus all who had various kinds of sickness, and laying his hands on each one, he healed them. Moreover, demons came out of many people, shouting, 'You are the Son of God!' But he rebuked them and would not allow them to speak, because they knew he was the Messiah."

When we read the short passage quickly, our takeaway might be that Jesus healed people and cast out demons. Yes, but read deeper. Let's look at what it specifically says: "laying his hands on each one." What picture of Jesus do we see in those words? He attended to people individually. He touched each one. He made it personal.

If we approach the miracles of Jesus believing these are events where the supernatural of God invades the natural order of creation, then seeing these cosmic events as one-on-one appointments Jesus had with each individual is all the more astonishing. Jesus offered His physical touch and healing spirit to each one. And He offers it to you.

There's more. As people were freed of their demonic oppression, those evil spirits cried out, "You are the Son of God!" That's a powerful statement about who Jesus is.

And it shows Jesus in His fullness—the human Jesus touching each person individually and the divine Jesus, the Son of God, whom the principalities and powers of the earth themselves testify to. All this was compressed into a few sentences.

As we explore some of Jesus's miracles in greater depth, we will be asking, "What does this miracle reveal about God? What does it show us about the person of Jesus?"

Miracles also draw us closer to Christ by revealing more about our character and the places in our character where we need to look more like Him.

In fact, when we read the miracles of Jesus—even much of Scripture—we often think of the events as things that happened way back then to *those people*. We look at the paralytic beside the Bethesda pool, the sad account of Lazarus's death and his sisters mourning, or the fishermen having a bad night with their nets, and we think of the miracles as Jesus helping *those people* back in *that time*.

But the miracles are about you and me as well. The man by the pool might have been paralyzed, but in what ways are we paralyzed too? Lazarus died and his sisters mourned. What is dead in our lives, and what are we mourning every day? The fishermen had worked all night but caught no fish. How is that like your life or mine when we have spent a lot of time working on something with little or no results, when our nets are empty too?

It's important to walk with the people Jesus healed and rescued and transformed. We find our miracle in the lives of those people Jesus entered into supernaturally.

This is not just a Bible study technique; it is actually a personal challenge. Are you willing to walk in someone else's shoes? Can you be open enough to see yourself in the condition of those whom Jesus encountered? Are you willing to be transparent enough that when you read about the paralytic or Lazarus or the fishermen, you can confess, "Yes, that's just like me"?

I believe if you will be open and vulnerable when you read Scripture, you will find your miracle, and you will see yourself in the transformational moment the miracle reveals.

The second principle of the Miracle Map is that the miracle you need most is just leading you to your greatest actual need—and that is a closer and deeper relationship with the Source of miracles.

MUD PIES AND MIRACLES

God works miracles in His time and in His way. This third principle in the Miracle Map really comes down to letting God be God.

Sometimes a miracle doesn't happen in the way we expect it. John 9 tells of Jesus's encounter with another blind man. His disciples asked Him a question about sickness and sin, and the blind man was probably standing there wondering if it was really necessary for them to have a philosophical discussion right then. I imagine he'd heard of the Healer and thought, *If this Jesus could just touch my eyes, I could see again.*

The discussion went on, and I'm sure the blind man was thinking, *Really, Jesus, I need You to touch me to help me see again.*

But what did Jesus do? He knelt to the ground, spit into the dirt, and formed some mud with His fingers. He then took these mud cakes and put them on both of the blind man's eyes, telling him to wash in the Siloam pool. The man did so, and the Bible says that "the man . . . came home seeing" (verse 7).

I bet the blind man, once he knew Jesus was in the area, might have expected that Jesus could help him see. I doubt he ever expected that Jesus would heal him by putting mud cakes on his eyes.

The miracle we're looking for might not be the miracle God gives us.

Christian music artist Natalie Grant and her husband, Bernie, wanted children, but were unable to conceive. Doctors gave them less than a 1 percent chance of ever getting pregnant. They prayed for a miracle. They tried fertility shots. But after dozens of shots, they still were unable to conceive.

Then after seventy-six fertility shots, Natalie's pregnancy test was positive. Their prayer was answered. And when Natalie had her first ultrasound, not one but two heartbeats were detected. Months later twin daughters were born.

But wait. She conceived again—this time unplanned. Natalie calls Sadie "the miracle I never asked for." Soon Natalie found herself in the midst of postpartum depression that would last nearly two years. Self-doubt, inadequacy, and guilt kept her in a very dark place.

Then, in one of the miracles of Jesus, Natalie found her strength. She turned to Matthew 14 and read about Jesus walking on water. Natalie realized God didn't stop the storm, but He was there for the disciples, with His comfort and His strength.

This passage marked the beginning of her recovery.[8]

So what was the miracle here? It started with a simple but fervent prayer for a miracle baby. God gave Natalie and Bernie the miracle they didn't expect—twins. And then another child—the miracle they "never asked for." And then, in the midst of her dark depression, Natalie found her miracle in the miracle of Jesus walking on water.

As we seek the miracle that God has for us, we will sometimes be surprised by a miracle we don't expect or didn't even know to ask for. It's essential we don't focus so much on the miracle we think we need that we miss the miracle God knows we really need. Often we ask Him to stop the storm, but the miracle He delivers is getting us through the storm.

There have been many married couples in our church who really wanted to have a child but were unable. They prayed for a miracle just as Natalie Grant did, but it seemed the heavens were silent. They would later find out God wasn't silent. He was just guiding them to a child who desperately needed them.

Through adoption, they found their miracle. Now, looking back, they see God's answer clearly and are so grateful for the miracle child He brought them. But it had been almost impossible to see that God had a plan when they were going through the valley.

God loves us so much, and He sees down the road. He knows what's best for us. It's just that sometimes we can't see what He's up to. Someone once told me, "When you can't see God's hand, you can trust His heart." Today you can trust His heart. As you pray for the miracle you need most, let God give you the miracle in His time and in His way.

It's Not About You

God's miracle in your life will always bring glory to Himself and point people to Christ.

The fourth principle of the Miracle Map is what it's all about. The whole point of a miracle is to point people to the source of miracles. That's why our motivation for wanting a miracle is important. Why do you want God to work that miracle in your life? Is it because your deepest desire is to see God glorified, or is it all about you?

Sometimes my prayer for a miracle is a good and godly request, but my motives aren't totally unselfish. God usually has to take me through a waiting period before He gives the miracle. And even though I think I'm waiting on God to give me the miracle, it's really that God is waiting on me. He's waiting for my character to match my calling. He's waiting for my motives to be pure. He's waiting for me to come to the place where I will give Him all the glory.

When God provides our miracle, it's tempting to grab our blessing, breathe a big sigh of relief, and settle back into our comfortable routine. But there's a danger in that. Scripture makes it clear that we are blessed in order to be a blessing. Let's take a look at another of Jesus's miracle to see how serious God is about our producing spiritual fruit that's consistent with our growth.

One day Jesus and His disciples were traveling from Bethany to Jerusalem. Jesus was hungry and saw a fig tree by the road, but on it He found no figs, only leaves. He said, "May you never bear fruit again!" and the tree withered immediately (Matthew 21:19).

The disciples were astonished! They had already seen Jesus heal the sick, raise the dead, and give sight to the blind. Yet the Bible says, "When the disciples saw this, they were amazed" (verse 20). The withering tree must have been incredibly dramatic to elicit such a response from guys who had been given front-row seats to so many miracles! Jesus certainly knew how to get the disciples' attention. He knew that His time on earth was growing short. In fact, Jesus would be crucified just a few days later. So He chose to use a powerful object lesson to teach His disciples.

It's important to know that on a fig tree the fruit and the leaves begin to grow about the same time. That means that if a fig tree has leaves, it should also have fruit. Jesus found a tree that gave the *appearance* of being productive, but it wasn't. The miracle He performed in response is a cautionary tale for all believers.

Those who follow Christ are often compared in Scripture to strong, healthy trees, trees that bear fruit.

> Blessed is the one
>> who does not walk in step with the wicked
> or stand in the way that sinners take
>> or sit in the company of mockers,
> but whose delight is in the law of the LORD,
>> and who meditates on his law day and night.
> That person is like a tree planted by streams of water,
>> which yields its fruit in season
> and whose leaf does not wither—
>> whatever they do prospers. (Psalm 1:1–3)

The fruit we are to produce is described in Paul's letter to the Galatians: "But the fruit of the Spirit is love, joy, peace, forbearance, kindness, goodness, faithfulness, gentleness and self-control. Against such things there is no law" (5:22–23).

If a fruit tree is provided with sunshine, water, and good soil with plenty of nutrients, it should naturally grow and produce fruit.

Just imagine that you are the owner of an orchard. First, you do the back-breaking work of preparing and tilling the soil. Next, you carefully plant your young seedlings. During droughts you haul water to keep the soil moist. When strong winds come, you stake their trunks to keep them upright. You painstakingly work to prevent insects from attacking the tender plants. Branches need pruning. Fertilizer needs to be added to the soil. When the roots become waterlogged after a flood, you rework the drainage system. Finally the young trees begin to mature! You begin to see buds on the limbs and can hardly wait to taste the delicious fruit. As you work in the orchard each day, your thoughts are filled with homemade cobblers and fresh-baked pies. You've given your all for these trees and paid for them in sweat, sore muscles, and callused hands. Finally the time has come to taste the fruits of your labor.

But hold it! Something's seriously wrong here! The trees are strong and leafy, but some have *no fruit*! Imposters! The barren trees are fine to look at, but the purpose of a fruit tree is to produce fruit! As the orchard owner you have a decision to make. Are you going to invest more of your attention, hard work, and resources in the trees that fail to produce fruit? Will you give them another year or two?

Many times in my life haven't produced fruit in proportion to God's provision. I'm so thankful the Lord is patient with me! The miracle of the fig tree reminds me, however, never to mistake patience for approval. We need to ask God to provide for our needs, but we are also to pray for the wisdom and discipline that will have our lives bursting with abundant spiritual fruit.

It's important to remember this fourth principle in the Miracle Map: God's miracle in your life will always bring Him glory and point people to Christ. Instead of just saying a quick thank-you after you receive a blessing from God, ask Him what He wants you to do with that blessing for His glory.

Instead of just saying, "Wow, God, thanks for getting me out of that mess" or "I'm so glad You took care of that problem," ask, "God, what do You want me to do differently because of the miracle You've given me? How can I bring glory to You and point people to You?"

PRINCIPLES OF THE MIRACLE MAP

As we explore some of the miracles of Jesus, these four principles will help focus our attention on what's important as we search to find our own miracle, the miracle we need right now. Again, these are the four principles:

1. God always starts with the miracle you need most.
2. The miracle you need most leads you to what you really need most—a deeper relationship with God.
3. God works the miracle in His time and in His way.
4. God's miracle in your life will always bring Him glory and point people to Christ.

I mentioned five principles, and, yes, there's one more, one that's so important we need to address it separately in the next chapter. But before we go any further, let's stop and thank the source of miracles, Jesus Christ. The Miracle Map always starts with Jesus and ends with Jesus. You are here, and so is He, and He is leading you to the X that marks the spot, to the treasure of a deep and rich love relationship with the Savior.

Promises for the Path

The mind of man plans his way,
but the LORD directs his steps.

Proverbs 16:9, NASB

I cry out to God Most High,
to God who will fulfill his purpose for me.

Psalm 57:2, NLT

Call to me and I will answer you and tell you great and unsearchable things you do not know.

Jeremiah 33:3

Whether you turn to the right or to the left, your ears will hear a voice behind you, saying, "This is the way; walk in it."

Isaiah 30:21

I will instruct you and teach you in the way you should go;
I will counsel you with my loving eye on you.

Psalm 32:8

So I say to you: Ask and it will be given to you; seek and you will find; knock and the door will be opened to you. For everyone who asks receives; the one who seeks finds; and to the one who knocks, the door will be opened.

Which of you fathers, if your son asks for a fish, will give him a snake instead? Or if he asks for an egg, will give him a scorpion? If you then, though you are evil, know how to give good gifts to your children, how much more will your Father in heaven give the Holy Spirit to those who ask him!

Luke 11:9–13

3

Positioning Yourself
for a Miracle

I have been driven many times upon my knees by the
overwhelming conviction that I had nowhere else to go.
My own wisdom and that of all about me seemed insuf-
ficient for that day.

—Abraham Lincoln

You will not have to fight this battle. Take up your
positions; stand firm and see the deliverance the LORD
will give you.

—2 Chronicles 20:17

I IMAGINE IT STARTED like every other day for Bartimaeus. And I mean like
every other day. Maybe you find yourself waking up to a day that's like every
other day. Same ol', same ol'. You're just going through the motions, desperately
needing a breakthrough, something to break you out of the rut you're in.

I imagine Bartimaeus woke up while it was still dark so he could get an early start. Being first to his usual spot was essential for surviving another day. He knew his route and had memorized every path and every turn in every narrow alleyway.

It didn't matter that it was still dark outside. He lived in a continual night because of his blindness.

The mention of his name is interesting. *Bar* means "son of," so he is literally "son of Timaeus." In many of Jesus's miracles, the names of people aren't mentioned, but this man's name is. So we might conclude there is something of note here. Some scholars suggest that the father, Timaeus, must have been well known in those parts. We can't confirm that, but we suspect Timaeus was known at least in the local community.

Yet even if Timaeus was well known, it appears that his son, Bartimaeus, had been somewhat forgotten. His blindness had reduced him to begging. While he may have been known in and around Jericho, it was in the context of pity and hopelessness, perhaps like the homeless guy with a sign at the stoplight on our way home from work. We know he's there, but we don't really see him or remember him. Likewise, people would say of Bartimaeus, "There's that guy again. What's his name? You know, Timaeus's son."

And then they'd just pass him by.

I'm sure Bartimaeus's goal each morning was to get to the best begging place in the city: beside the road to the marketplace. He needed to get an early start so he could be the first one to that spot. As he sat in his familiar place, he began to feel the warmth of the sun on his face. He knew the sun was rising. He began to hear the *clippety-clop* of the donkeys' hooves as they pulled their wagons filled with vegetables to market. Then Bartimaeus could make out the voices of people bartering in the marketplace. Soon there were sounds of children laughing and playing. The crowds got bigger, just as they always did, and the chatter of people grew louder as the dawn gave way to day.

Yet this day something was different. Bartimaeus couldn't pinpoint the difference, but he noticed it. He knew. He could hear it. In the air. In the sounds. In people's voices. What was going on? More people began to gather, more than usual. There was more movement than usual bustling by him on the road.

I can just imagine Bartimaeus calling out, "What's happening?" I'm sure nobody bothered to answer him, because he was invisible to everyone. I imagine he finally grabbed someone by the cloak, pulled him close, and said, "Tell me! What's going on?"

And someone must have said, "Jesus of Nazareth."

Jesus of Nazareth is happening.

I believe Bartimaeus had heard about Jesus and His ability to heal. Jesus's presence in the city of Jericho must have filled Bartimaeus with hope. And hope was something he perhaps hadn't known for most of his life. Yet hope sprang up within his soul because he had heard how Jesus of Nazareth had healed the lame and the sick and made blind eyes see.

THE MIRACLE SPOT

In addition to the previous four principles of the Miracle Map, there is one more principle, and this account of Bartimaeus is a great illustration of it. Quite simply, it's this: *Only God can provide a miracle, but you have to put yourself in position to receive it.*

The Source of miracles was passing by where Bartimaeus always went to beg. When Bartimaeus settled into his familiar place earlier that morning, he had no idea that he was in the perfect spot to receive a miracle that day.

Bartimaeus may not have been aware of his *physical* position along the path that day, but I believe he had developed a heart position, a *spiritual* posture, that made him ready to receive the miracle Jesus had for him. The Bible tells us that we can prepare ourselves spiritually to have that same heart posture to receive a miracle.

Now I need to be careful here. Just as you and I can't earn salvation, which comes only through faith in what Christ did for us on the cross, we can't earn a miracle. Miracles and all of God's blessings are gifts of His grace. We can't earn a miracle or do anything to deserve a miracle, but we can put our hearts in a posture to receive a miracle from God.

There is a miracle mentioned in the Old Testament that really opened my eyes to this Miracle Map principle of positioning.

The godly king of Judah and his nation were being attacked by three kings and their three armies. It was three against one. It wasn't a fair fight. But God revealed to the king of Judah that a miracle was on the way. God said to the king, "You will not have to fight this battle. Take up your positions; stand firm and see the deliverance the LORD will give you. . . . Do not be afraid; do not be discouraged. Go out to face them tomorrow, and the LORD will be with you" (2 Chronicles 20:17).

Did you catch that? God told the people of Judah, "Take up your positions." God was telling them, "It's not your job to fight the battle and win a miraculous victory. That's My job. Your job is not to conjure up a miracle. Your job is to put yourself in position to receive the miracle I have for you."

The same is true for you. You don't have to struggle for God's miracles and blessings. You don't have to earn God's miracles and blessings. You just have to prepare yourself. Put your heart in position for the miracle. Then stand firm on God's promises.

I truly believe that Bartimaeus didn't just put himself physically in the perfect spot for a miracle, but more important, he put his heart in position to receive the miracle that day. You and I can learn several specific things from this blind beggar about how to put our hearts in the right place to receive the miracle we need most.

The Scriptures tell us there are three heart steps that will take us directly to the X that marks the spot for a miracle. Humility, honor, and faith are the major components that make up our part in receiving God's miracle in our lives.

THE PATH OF HUMILITY

The first step to the place where God gives His miracles is a step onto the path of humility. That's because our pride blocks God's power in our lives. We can't be full of Christ when we're full of ourselves.

Many times God has had to knock the pride out of my life so He could bring me to the place where I admitted I needed a miracle. The place of humility could more appropriately be called the place of desperation, the place where there is nowhere else to look but up, the place where we're at the end of our rope.

As Jesus said in His Sermon on the Mount, "You're blessed when you're at the end of your rope. With less of you there is more of God and his rule" (Matthew 5:3, MSG). God takes hold when we finally let go.

Bartimaeus knew he was in a desperate situation and needed a divine change. No one had to tell him that. Mark's gospel says, "When he heard that it was Jesus of Nazareth, he began to shout, 'Jesus, Son of David, have mercy on me!'" (10:47).

Note the phrase "have mercy on me." Bartimaeus knew he needed mercy. You see, everyone else in the crowd that day was as desperate as Bartimaeus. They just didn't realize it. They needed mercy as much as Bartimaeus did. They just didn't know it.

Every one of us is desperate for change. But many of us don't know it. Many of us won't admit it.

We can't change the self-destructive habits and patterns that have devastating consequences in our lives—not without God's power—but many of us think we can. We can't get out of the ruts in our lives without God's deliverance, but we think we can.

Many of us think, *Well, sure, I have some issues, but I'm okay. Sure, I need to make a little change here, a little change there. And, yeah, my schedule is overloaded. I need to do this. I need to do that. I need to make a few changes. But these are just little adjustments. I'll get to them. I'm kind of in a valley, but*

I'll get out of it. I'll just try this new thing, change a little habit, start a new routine.

No, we *all* need drastic and divine change. You and I can't change anything in our lives without God's power. We can't get out of our ruts by relying on our own trivial fixes. We will never get out of the valley by our own feeble efforts. On our own, life is long and dry and hopeless. We're desperate without God's power.

In fact, we're all just as desperate as this poor, blind beggar, but most of us don't realize it or admit it. We're just as blind as Bartimaeus. We're blinded by our pride. We're blinded to the fact that we are desperate for a miracle. And the only way to receive a miracle is to humbly admit that we desperately need one.

The journey to the place of miracles always starts on the path of humility. Scripture says, "God opposes the proud but shows favor to the humble" (James 4:6). We can't earn God's blessings, but we can choose the path of humility that will put us in position to receive God's miracles in our lives.

SET ASIDE YOUR PRIDE

When Bartimaeus embraced his desperation and called out to Jesus, the Bible says, "Many rebuked him and told him to be quiet" (Mark 10:48).

Maybe the crowds were embarrassed by this beggar, and their pride led them to push him into the background and to silence him. It's as if they were saying, "Be quiet. You're embarrassing yourself, Bartimaeus, and you're embarrassing us. You're embarrassing the whole city of Jericho. This great healer and teacher is coming through, and we want to make a good impression. We finally get a celebrity in town. We don't need you yelling over the crowd. We need to give this Jesus a chance to talk. So just sit down, shut up, and stay in your place. Stay in your little rut. Be quiet." Bartimaeus wouldn't have received his miracle if he had worried about what everyone thought of him.

We sometimes hear those discouraging words ourselves. We hear from those whose lives are going so well (or at least that's what they claim), and we see people who appear to have it all together. Perhaps some in our lives "play the spiritual card," suggesting to us in one way or another that we must be doing something wrong to have struggled for so long. Messages, spoken and postured, serve to silence us, to make our confession of desperation seem unseemly and embarrassing.

But I love what Bartimaeus did. He just yelled louder. After a lifetime of being forgotten, dismissed, overlooked, and treated as if he were invisible, he had the courage to cry out and reach out to Jesus. How great is that! Bartimaeus set aside all those negative voices and discouraging words. He set aside the prideful-ness of the crowd and his own pride, and he called out to God again. Only louder. "Son of David, have mercy on me!"

By embracing his desperation and not letting pride (his own or the crowd's) deter him, Bartimaeus sought his miracle. He wouldn't let the crowds determine his future. He was determined to connect with Jesus of Nazareth, the Son of God.

So here's the question for you and me. Do you really want to find your miracle? Or are you too proud to admit your desperate need? Is your future shaped by the pressure of the crowd or by other Christians posturing seemingly perfect lives?

What will it take for you to shout, with blind Bartimaeus, "Son of David, have mercy on me!"?

WORTH IT FOR ONE

Many times in the history of Woodlands Church, God has led us to places of desperation and dead ends so He could lead us to the place of miracles.

More than twenty years ago, when we followed God's nudge to move to The Woodlands, Texas, and start a church, we knew we desperately needed God. We just didn't realize how desperately we needed Him!

We told everybody we could about our new church plant and how exciting it would be. Fifteen people showed up at our first gathering. I told them how this church would be all about Jesus and not about religion. I preached what I thought was a good sermon and invited them to come back the next week and to invite friends.

Well, apparently not all of them were as excited as we were because only eight of them came back the next week—and five of those were our family! That's when we first realized how desperate we really were for God's miracle to build His church.

We were so discouraged, and we began to question God's call to step out in faith and start the church. We had very little money, no place to meet, and now only eight members. But in that desperation we humbly admitted how much we needed God. The Lord met us in our desperation and clearly impressed upon our hearts that He would do the miracle of building His church and that all we had to do was put ourselves in position to receive His power and strength.

We felt the Lord asking us, *If just one person comes to know Me and that person's life is transformed and eternal destiny is changed, won't it all be worth it?*

It was so true. If God did one miracle and changed one life and nothing else through Woodlands Church, it would all be worth it. The greatest miracle God works is the miracle of transforming a life and changing an eternal destiny. And only God can transform a life.

That took the pressure off us as we put the focus on God. We had been reminded that it's not our church, it's God's church, and it's God's job to grow His church.

For the next two months, we gathered with our eight members to pray and plan the first public celebration service that would kick off Woodlands Church. We spent every dime we had on renting a facility, purchasing the equipment we needed, and sending out invitations to the community. We said if just one person came into a personal relationship with Christ and then the church had to fold up and close its doors, it would still be worth it. It would all be worth it for one miracle of a changed life.

We prayed for God to work that miracle and to build His church, and God answered our prayer. One hundred and sixty-four people came to the first service, and four of them prayed to receive Christ, and their eternal destiny was changed!

Over the past two decades, God has built and grown Woodlands Church with thousands of miracles of lives changed forever by His transformative grace. It's not our church. It's God's church and God's job to grow His church however He chooses. All we've been doing for the last twenty years is seeking to be faithful week after week to pray and prepare for one more person to come to Christ, for God to work one more miracle of life change.

Whenever I forget this truth, God always knocks my pride out from under me so I come face to face with my powerlessness and get back on the path of humility that takes me to His miracle.

THE POWER OF HONOR

After you're emptied of pride and have stepped onto the path of humility, realizing how desperately you need a miracle, the next step toward a miracle is to give honor to God.

There is an honor system that God has set up as a universal principle. His honor system sets in motion the full, undeserved blessing of God. Honor is a key in unlocking the miracles of God in our lives.

In Mark 6 we see that Jesus went back to His hometown of Nazareth. He was preaching in the synagogue, and people were amazed at His teaching. Someone said, "Wait a minute. Isn't that the Jesus who grew up here in Nazareth? Isn't that Mary's son? He grew up down the street from me. His brothers and sisters went to Nazareth High with my kids. He's no big deal. I remember he worked with his dad in the carpenter shop down the street. In fact, honey, I think Jesus built our kitchen table, didn't he? Isn't that the guy who built our kitchen table? Yeah. He's nothing special." And look at what Jesus said about His hometown: "A prophet is not without honor except in his own town, among his relatives and in his own home." As a result, Mark reported that Jesus "could not do any miracles there, except lay his hands on a few sick people and heal them" (verses 4–5).

It says the people refused to honor Jesus, and it kept Him from doing all the miracles He wanted to do. Just think about that for a moment. It doesn't say that He would not do any miracles there. It says, "He could not do any miracles there except lay his hands on a few sick people and heal them."

I would understand if He wouldn't do any miracles because they didn't honor Him. It would make sense that Jesus would think, *Hey, if you're not going to honor Me, then I choose not to do any miracles for you.*

But that's not what happened. Scripture doesn't say Jesus *wouldn't* do any miracles. It says He *couldn't* do many miracles there. And as hard as that may be to believe, that's what the text says.

That shows me that God has set up His honor system, and when He walked this earth, He placed Himself in it to show us that dishonor blocks the miracles of God in our lives. On the other hand, honoring Him opens up the full blessings of God in our lives.

I'm not saying you and I can ever deserve God's miracle by honoring Him. I'm saying Scripture is real clear that honoring God and others puts us in the right place to receive an undeserved miracle from God. So if honor is so important, what is it? The Hebrew word for "honor" is *kabad,* and it literally means "weight or heaviness." To honor someone, then, is to give weight, importance, seriousness, and value to them.

To honor God means I give Him the importance, value, and seriousness that He demands and deserves in my life. The Hebrew root of the word for "dishonor" pictures an early morning mist, a light fog that you can brush away with your hand. Mist has no heaviness or lasting value.

Therefore, I dishonor God when I treat Him as if I can just brush Him off as unimportant in my life. To honor God means that I first recognize who He is and give Him His rightful place in my life. The place of priority.

We even see God's honor system come to life in the story of Bartimaeus. He was giving honor to Christ and putting himself in a place to receive a miracle when he cried out, "Jesus, Son of David, have mercy on me!" And the words "Son of David" are very revealing.

Every Jew in the crowd that day knew the prophecies that the Messiah was to come through the lineage of David. Most of the people in the crowd either didn't believe or just weren't convinced that Jesus was the Messiah they had been waiting for. The Pharisees and other religious leaders watching Jesus pass through Jericho that day didn't believe He was the Messiah and were doing everything they could to dishonor Him in the peoples' eyes.

So when Bartimaeus cried out, "Jesus, Son of David," he was saying, "I believe, Jesus, that You are the Messiah. I believe You are the Son of God. I believe You are not just a great prophet or a great teacher or a big celebrity walking through town. I also believe You're more than a miracle worker. I believe You are God!"

What a powerful truth. What an essential truth. Bartimaeus positioned himself to receive an undeserved miracle by declaring who Jesus rightfully was.

His declaration of honor, giving Jesus His rightful and weighty title, showed that this blind man had a clearer vision of who Jesus was than all those in the crowd who had twenty-twenty vision.

It's my prayer that God will open your eyes to who Jesus really is and that you'll give Him first place, His rightful place of honor, in your life.

The Bible tells us in Proverbs to "honor GOD with everything you own; give him the first and the best" (3:9, MSG).

As a Christ follower, I can honor God daily by giving Him the first and best of my life. He deserves the first and best, not the last and worst. Notice that it says to honor God "with everything you own."

When we think of everything we own, we usually think only of finances and material possessions. I'm sure this scripture includes finances, but it pertains to so much more than that.

"Everything you own" means everything God has given you—your gifts, talents, time, and resources. Let's make this real practical. I honor God at my workplace when I give my best, when I make an all-out effort, using my gifts and abilities to their full potential. I dishonor God at work when I give a half-hearted effort. That's why the scripture says, "Whatever work you do, do it with all your heart. Do it for the Lord and not for men" (Colossians 3:23, NLV).

So whenever you do anything, you honor God when you do it with all your heart. You can honor God by washing dishes and taking out the garbage if you do it with all your heart.

My best efforts by themselves could never bring about a miracle, but when I give my best to God—no matter how insignificant the task might seem—God can use it to bring about a miracle. God used a small boy's lunch to feed five thousand people because he was willing to honor Christ by giving all he had.[9]

BELIEVING IS SEEING

Bartimaeus had no idea when he sat down in his everyday spot as the sun was coming up that he had positioned himself in the perfect place to meet the Miracle Maker as He passed through Jericho. Much more important, however, Bartimaeus had positioned his heart to receive the miracle that he needed most. In crying out "Jesus, Son of David, have mercy on me!" Bartimaeus humbly revealed his desperation for Jesus and powerfully declared his honor of Jesus.

Humility and honor led Bartimaeus to the place where he took the last step that put his heart in line for the miracle. The step of faith.

The passage goes on:

Jesus stopped and said, "Call him."

So they called to the blind man, "Cheer up! On your feet! He's calling you." Throwing his cloak aside, he jumped to his feet and came to Jesus.

"What do you want me to do for you?" Jesus asked him.

The blind man said, "Rabbi, I want to see."

"Go," said Jesus, "your faith has healed you." Immediately he received his sight and followed Jesus along the road. (Mark 10:49–52)

I love this: "Jesus stopped and said, 'Call him.'"

What must this prideful crowd have thought? This blind beggar who was so embarrassing to everyone was the very one who stopped Jesus of Nazareth in His tracks. And Jesus called specifically for him. Perhaps some thought, *Okay, now the rabbi will rebuke him. He's gonna get his.* Others said to Bartimaeus, "Cheer up! . . . He's calling you." We don't know how this was said, but given the context, I think some were saying this sarcastically or condescendingly: "Cheer up, little beggar man. You finally got the Rabbi's attention. Can't wait to watch this."

But Bartimaeus was all in. He threw his cloak aside and stood before Jesus. And the crowd must have gasped when Jesus asked Bartimaeus, "What do you want me to do for you?"

Oh my. Suddenly the crowd was put back in its place. Suddenly that pride had burst and shriveled up like a popped balloon. And now this embarrassing Bartimaeus would have a personal meeting with Jesus.

Bartimaeus answered Jesus simply: "Rabbi, I want to see." He expressed his deepest need to the Son of God, because Bartimaeus believed He could heal him. And Jesus said, "Go, your faith has healed you."

In that moment Bartimaeus found his miracle. Suddenly his night turned to day. Suddenly he could see.

Jesus's words grab my heart: "Go, your faith has healed you." Bartimaeus's faith in Christ activated the miracle. I certainly don't understand how my faith and God's miracles come together, but I know that my faith is essential to putting me in position to receive the miracle.

Over and over Jesus would tell people, "Be it done to you according to your faith."

Jesus was saying that when I put my faith in Him, He takes me to the place of miracles. By the way, Jesus also made it clear that it's not the amount of faith that makes the difference when He said that I can have faith as small as a mustard seed and move mountains (see Matthew 17:20).

Jesus told us that it's not the amount of our faith that matters; it's the object of our faith that makes all the difference.

Your faith is only as good as the One you put your faith in. Don't put your faith in a miracle. Put your faith in Jesus, who can work miracles. Bartimaeus took the little bit of faith he had and placed it all on Jesus to work a miracle in his life.

When it comes to miracles, a lot of people in modern-day society say, "I'll believe it when I see it." But God says, "You'll see it when you believe it." For Bartimaeus and for us, *believing comes before seeing.*

I believe Jesus is calling you out of your darkness. Jesus has stopped among the crowd and said, "Call him. Call her." He is calling you. And He's asking what you want Him to do for you.

I believe you need to throw off your cloak as Bartimaeus did. Commentators say that this is a symbol of Bartimaeus's leaving behind all he had in order to follow Jesus. I believe that too often we remain out of position for a miracle because we want to continue to be the driver of our lives. We want to maintain control of the car we're in and not let go of the wheel in faith.

I believe you need to say simply and specifically to Jesus, right now, what your need is, just as Bartimaeus did. Confess to Jesus your greatest need. Allow yourself to really believe that Jesus, the Son of God, the doer of miracles, can work a miracle in your life.

Ask the Lord to guide you along the path of humility, honor, and faith so you'll be ready to receive all that God wants to give you.

Promises for Building Your Faith

Let us come boldly to the throne of our gracious God. There we will receive his mercy, and we will find grace to help us when we need it most.

Hebrews 4:16, NLT

I will do whatever you ask in my name, so that the Father may be glorified in the Son.

John 14:13

This is the confidence we have in approaching God: that if we ask anything according to his will, he hears us. And if we know that he hears us—whatever we ask—we know that we have what we asked of him.

1 John 5:14–15

Jesus replied, "I am the bread of life. Whoever comes to me will never be hungry again. Whoever believes in me will never be thirsty."

John 6:35, NLT

Humble yourselves before the Lord, and he will lift you up.

James 4:10

Humble yourselves under the mighty power of God, and at the right time he will lift you up in honor.

1 Peter 5:6, NLT

He has shown you, O mortal, what is good.

　　And what does the LORD require of you?

To act justly and to love mercy

　　and to walk humbly with your God.

Micah 6:8

Truly I tell you, if you have faith as small as a mustard seed, you can say to this mountain, "Move from here to there," and it will move. Nothing will be impossible for you.

Matthew 17:20

Jesus: The Healer

How sweet the name of Jesus sounds, in a believer's ear. It soothes his sorrows, heals his wounds, and drives away his fear.

—John Newton

Christ is the Good Physician. There is no disease He cannot heal; no sin He cannot remove; no trouble He cannot help.

—James H. Aughey

4

When You're Stuck

Jesus Heals a Paralyzed Man

Afterward Jesus returned to Jerusalem for one of the
Jewish holy days. Inside the city, near the Sheep Gate, was
the pool of Bethesda, with five covered porches. Crowds
of sick people—blind, lame, or paralyzed—lay on the
porches. One of the men lying there had been sick for
thirty-eight years. When Jesus saw him and knew he had
been ill for a long time, he asked him, "Would you like to
get well?"

"I can't, sir," the sick man said, "for I have no one to
put me into the pool when the water bubbles up. Someone
else always gets there ahead of me."

Jesus told him, "Stand up, pick up your mat, and
walk!"

Instantly, the man was healed! He rolled up his
sleeping mat and began walking!

—John 5:1–9, NLT

THE ASSOCIATION OF WATER with special healing has a long history.

The ancient Romans were famous for their baths. They built amazing spas out of stone that surrounded hot springs, which created sauna-like pools. The Roman Empire eventually extended far north across Europe and into Great Britain. One city in Great Britain was built by the Romans around hot springs. The whole city was created as a steamy bath. The name of the city? Well, they called it Bath: Bath, England.

In the late 1800s and early 1900s, America became obsessed with the healing powers of fresh air and hot springs. It was before a cure for tuberculosis had been found, and those afflicted with this lung disease were often advised to get away from the filthy, smoggy cities and to go into the wilderness for fresh air and clean water. Native Americans had reportedly found hot springs in the West, and many Americans sought the promise of the natural waters of Colorado and New Mexico. At one time, residents of Denver flocked to Colorado Springs for its healing powers—even though Colorado Springs never actually had hot springs.

Today "healing pools" take the form of enhanced Jacuzzis, backyard pools, and portable spas—all promising health benefits and even healing from all sorts of aches and pains. I'm told healing pools even pop up as elements of certain computer games, such as *Half-Life* and *Minecraft*. Apparently healing pools are a thing.

The ancient Roman spas probably offered a degree of real healthfulness, and I can well believe that the hot springs of the Wild West effectively relieved some symptoms of TB. Even the healing pools of today possibly have some benefits for those in ill health. I know a good hot tub usually makes me feel pretty relaxed!

Of course, associated with all of these is the idea of magical properties, of amazing powers for transformation, of miraculous healing of bodies racked by disease, cancer, or paralysis. It was the promise then, and it is the promise today, of all sorts of things—special oils, natural waters, and healing pools.

That's the background for this scriptural account of the Bethesda pool. This hot spring, on the outskirts of Jerusalem, was reported to have special healing powers.

For hundreds of years scholars thought the Bethesda pool never actually existed, claiming there was no evidence for it. They believed this biblical story was complete fiction. But in the 1800s archaeologists were exploring an area to the south of an old church, and further excavation clearly revealed a pool—in the very place that Scripture claimed this Bethesda pool to be. When you go to the Holy Land and visit these areas, in many cases you're not really walking on the same paths where Jesus walked, because you're walking a hundred feet *above* where Jesus walked. Over time the topography has changed, and people have built on top of the original locations. But this is a spot where they've dug down to the level of two thousand years ago. I've had the privilege of standing right next to the pool of Bethesda where Jesus performed this miracle, where Jesus actually stood.

I think there's a lesson in this for all of us. How many times has the Bible been questioned? Disbelieved? Even ridiculed? And yet how many times has something been discovered or uncovered or recovered to prove the doubters wrong and the Bible right?

This Bethesda pool is interesting for another reason. It's the mystery of a missing Scripture verse. That's right. If you look at any recent version of the Bible—say the New International Version, English Standard Version, or The Living Bible—you'll find that verse 4 is missing, and in its place is a footnote marker. If you go back to the King James Version, though, you will find verse 4 there in its entirety. What's going on? Are people tampering with the Bible?

Not really.

Bible scholars have determined that verse 4 actually describes the popular superstition of the times that had created the mystique surrounding the Bethesda pool. Recent Bible translations have made this information a footnote so we can know about the superstition but not consider it to be officially part of the text of God's Word.

This "footnote verse" says: "For an angel went down at a certain season into the pool, and troubled the water: whosoever then first after the troubling of the water stepped in was made whole of whatsoever disease he had" (John 5:4, KJV). Again, modern translations suggest this was the legend of the Bethesda pool, making it clear that it wasn't actually an angel from God who did this.

In other words, the sick, the lame, and the paralyzed made their way to the Bethesda pool because it was thought to be a source for healing. It was thought that when the waters swirled and bubbled and spouted, an angel had made that happen, and the first person to enter the pool after the waters had been troubled would be healed.

All these sick people were lined up, trying to be the first one into the pool when the waters were troubled so they could be healed. Being second wouldn't work, according to the superstition. You had to be first.

This is the plight of the paralytic man when we encounter him in John 5. He isn't given a name. He's identified only by the length of time he's been an invalid: thirty-eight years. As a paralytic, he needs help; he cannot get into the pool on his own.

The great Bible teacher Ray Stedman wrote: "The facts, of course, are that the pool of Bethesda, like many similar pools in the Jerusalem area, is an intermittent spring. At times water is released in surges from hidden reservoirs in the hills around the city, causing these springs to rise and fall suddenly. This is what gave rise to the superstition about an angel troubling the pool."[10]

Stedman went on to say, "Undoubtedly healings did occur there." He suggested that some of these healings were psychological, and I tend to agree. Maybe the minerals in the waters provided physical improvement for some people. Or maybe the angel of the Lord appeared, and there were indeed some supernatural miracles happening there.

When you believe in miracles, you never count God out.

The fact is, I don't know if the pool healed people or not. I don't know if the

Roman baths or Colorado Springs or today's "healing pools" have natural healing properties or if God works through some of these natural forms to perform
supernatural healing.

What I do know is that this paralytic man believed the pool could heal him.
And he was in a bind, because he couldn't know when the waters would move,
and he had no one to carry him to the water when it did.

This wasn't Old Faithful—that geyser in Yellowstone National Park that
erupts every hour or so. This was Bethesda pool, and we don't know when the
springs would bubble, when an angel supposedly would stir the waters. Maybe
it was once a week or once a month. We don't know. But we can imagine the
desperation of the paralytic man who has been unable to get into the pool for a
very long time.

However, on this particular day Jesus walked into his world.

WHAT HAS PARALYZED YOU?

Psychologists use the term "escape paralysis" to describe a special phenomenon.
You're watching a television show or movie in which someone is kidnapped. The
kidnapper leaves the place where the person is being held, and you start to root
for the captive to get out, to run, to get away. If you're like me, you shout out
loud at the screen, "Run!!!"

And yet the person doesn't move. Of course, sometimes the show has another forty-five minutes to go, and the producers have to keep the captive where
he is. That's when it gets cheesy. But at other times the story is depicting a real
phenomenon. Sometimes captives, hostages, and prisoners choose not to escape
physically because they feel bound emotionally to their circumstances.

Sometimes we suffer from this kind of paralysis in life. We find ourselves
trapped in life situations—at home, in our workplace, maybe even in church.
We know we need to change things. We know we're in a rut. We know we need
to escape whatever is holding us back.

But we don't leave.

I don't know about the paralytic man at Bethesda pool. I'm not saying he had a chance to escape his condition. But I do know he had been stuck in a hopeless situation for thirty-eight years, and he needed a miracle to get unstuck. He needed a miracle to lift him off the mat.

Is this the kind of miracle you need?

Some people are paralyzed *relationally*. Sharon is a young woman who keeps falling for the wrong kind of men. She gets into a relationship with a guy, only to realize at some point that he's a poser or a user or an abuser. She breaks up with him, but she makes the same mistake the next time. She's stuck in a relationship cycle. She can't seem to break free from the paralysis.

A lot of people today are paralyzed *emotionally*. George struggles with fear. He finds himself retreating from challenges at work, afraid he might lose his job if he fails. His fear also plagues him at home, where he shrinks from responsibility and doesn't take the lead on anything. He and his wife are okay, but she wishes he would be more adventurous. But George can't bring himself to step out, take a risk, or try something new. His fear paralyzes him and keeps him from walking confidently through life.

Some people are paralyzed *financially*. I know a couple who always live beyond their means. They crave the good life, and they buy as much of it as they can, yet they don't have the income to cover their expenses. When they find themselves in enormous debt, they take out loans, restructure their debts, and slowly dig their way out. But before long they make the same mistakes all over again. They're stuck in a financial rut.

I know many who are paralyzed *spiritually*. We all need to grow spiritually, but I know some who always seem to struggle with the same aspect of faith—prayer, devotion, church, time with God. They're stagnated in their spiritual growth, dealing with the same issues for years, even decades, like this paralyzed man. The same character defects, bad habits, and sins hold them back. They never seem to break through to a new level.

Psychologists will tell you that one of the dynamics of escape paralysis is that the captive may develop a bond with the kidnapper. They call it trauma bonding, and one form of this is the Stockholm syndrome, when a captive begins to identify with and feel emotionally sympathetic toward the captor. The most famous public case of this was back in the seventies with Patty Hearst. She was kidnapped and held captive, but she later joined her captors and assisted them in robberies. It was determined that she had developed this kind of sympathetic bonding with the people who had captured her.

A similar kind of bonding occurs in our lives as well. We sometimes bond with the sin in our lives. Our daily rebellions, our selfish behaviors, our compulsive addictions become not only those things that hold us captive; they become the things we hold on to and bond with, sometimes deeply.

Sin has taken us. It has captured our hearts and lives, and now we feel bonded to it.

So we are paralyzed in our lives, perhaps relationally or emotionally or spiritually—or all three of them. We feel stuck in these sin bondages we're holding on to.

But then it happens. On this particular day, Jesus walks into our world.

Do You Want to Get Well?

In John 5:1–9, Jesus uttered four phrases. All four of them are surprising, bold, and even shocking. The first phrase perhaps most of all.

"Would you like to get well?" Jesus asked the paralytic.

We're surprised when He asks this, because the answer appears to be obvious. This paralytic had begged for help to get into the pool for quite some time. Of course he wanted to get well. Or did he?

We don't know. We can assume that Jesus knew something about this man that we don't. Some commentators suggest that Jesus knew there was more going on with this man than met the eye.

After all, there is more going on with you and me—our private paralysis, our secret sins that have taken us captive—than other people know.

If you need a miracle today, then these words are for you. Jesus is asking you, challenging you, "Would you like to get well?"

Our quick answer is "Of course, Lord. Of course I want to get well! Isn't that obvious? Help me into the healing water, please!" We reach out toward Jesus with one hand yet hold on to our bondage with the other. Don't you think Jesus sees that and knows that about us? Don't you think He is asking us if we want to get well because He knows, in fact, we really don't?

Is it possible that you're paralyzed by a kind of comfort zone of sin and self, your own escape paralysis within a life you secretly love? Is it possible that the life you lead, the sins you commit, and the addictions you harbor are holding you firmly in their bonds?

So many times in Scripture we see Jesus encountering people who are paralyzed in their condition and inviting them to step out of it. When he encountered the Samaritan woman, she asked Him, "Give me this [living] water so that I won't get thirsty" (John 4:15). It was her version of saying, "Help me into the healing pool."

He replied with a trick comment, "Go, call your husband" (verse 16).

She replied that she had no husband.

Then Jesus responded by identifying her escape paralysis, the sin she held on to, the compulsive pattern that had sabotaged her life: "You are right when you say you have no husband. The fact is, you have had five husbands, and the man you now have is not your husband" (verses 17–18).

Jesus named her bondage, and He called her out of it.

And He is calling you out of your bondage as well. Right now. "Would you like to get well?"

He is saying that you need to let go. You need to let go of whatever paralyzes you. You need to let go of those husbands you keep marrying to try to fill the hole in your life. You need to let go of your sin that gives you a comfort zone but steals your life.

Yes, Jesus is calling you out.

"Would you like to get well?"

STAND UP

It was a bold thing to say to the paralytic, but Jesus did not hesitate.

"Stand up," Jesus told him.

Now we can interpret Jesus's intention here in a number of ways. But my two cents is that Jesus was saying, "Stop making excuses." He was telling the paralyzed man to stop his life as a paralytic and to start a new life as one who had been healed.

Again, we don't know what the paralytic was thinking. We might dare put words in his mouth: *What? Stand up? You've got to be kidding me! If I could stand up, I wouldn't need You to help me into the pool! You're making fun of me now!*

We don't know if those were his thoughts, but we might think those things if we were in his condition.

And we are.

Think about it. We're looking for a miracle, we're paralyzed, and we see this man Jesus, and He tells us, "Stand up!"

What? Stand up? You've got to be kidding me! I'm paralyzed relationally, Lord! I'm emotionally bound up. I'm trapped in this problem I'm facing. Can't You see that these are holding me down? I can't stand up!

But Jesus keeps saying the same thing to us: "Stand up. Stop making excuses."

I believe standing up is the action that activates the miracle. In your case and mine, Jesus is saying, "Get off the ground. Get out of the gutter. Get up from the dirt. Stand up."

And I believe that when we obey, when we stand up, we are acting in faith, and a miracle starts to unfold. Principle five in the Miracle Map reminds us that only God works miracles, but He allows our faith to play a part in receiving a miracle.

Now I can well imagine that the paralytic man's first attempt to stand up was shaky. It was probably the most awkward, unnatural thing he had ever attempted. After all, he had been lying down for thirty-eight years. What might it have looked like? I'm sure his legs were weak and atrophied. I'm sure he struggled to his feet.

And so it is with us. Many times we think that as soon as we ask God for that miracle, then everything is going to happen instantly, and all the barriers will fall away. We think that everything will feel natural and come easily, that everything will just fall into place perfectly.

Nothing could be further from the truth.

You see, God asks us to stand up, and sometimes it's awkward. It feels unnatural to step out in faith, to follow Him. But whenever we do that, He opens the door for the miracle. It's amazing how He does it.

My tendency is to say, "God, I pray that You will just open that door, and then I'll step through it." But God replies, "No, you take a first step, and then I'll open the door." That's the way God works.

Remember in the Old Testament when God called Joshua to lead the people of Israel across the Jordan River and into the Promised Land? God said, "Tomorrow you're going into the Promised Land." There was just one problem. The Jordan River was at flood stage, flowing so fast they would all drown. Even so, God said, "I want you to put the priests up front, and I want them to walk into the water. As soon as they do, I'll work the miracle." I would have wanted God to work the miracle first. Then I would have had the courage to walk into the river. But God said, "You have to get your feet wet first."

As soon as the priests' feet touched the water, it parted. (See Joshua 3.)

That's the way God works. He says, "Stand up" or "Step in." The miracle you're looking for may begin right then.

So stand up or step in.

PICK UP YOUR MAT

The paralyzed man had probably used this mat his entire life. We assume he didn't own much of anything except this square of padding, a ratty old portable bed. And while someone might have given him a newer mat along the way, this was likely his only real possession for many years.

This man with a mat reminds me of someone else—a cartoon character with a blanket.

In 2015 *A Charlie Brown Christmas* aired for the fiftieth time. The story is familiar to us: Charlie Brown is so frustrated by the commercialization of the holiday that he finally shouts, "Isn't there anyone who knows what Christmas is all about?" Linus, hearing his friend's question, carries his blanket onstage and, under a spotlight, recites part of the Christmas story from the Bible, including these words: "Fear not: for, behold, I bring you good tidings of great joy, which shall be to all people. For unto you is born this day in the city of David a Saviour, which is Christ the Lord" (Luke 2:10–11, KJV). After Linus finishes, he walks back to his friend and says, "That's what Christmas is all about, Charlie Brown."

Jason Soroski in an online article told how this Charlie Brown special had been a standard part of his life growing up, but it was only as an adult that he noticed something in it for the first time.

Linus's blanket was, of course, a security blanket, his ever-present cloth companion. In all the Charlie Brown cartoons, Linus was never without it. But at the moment Linus recites the Bible verse "Fear not . . . a Savior, which is Christ the Lord," he drops his precious blanket.

Soroski doesn't believe that was an accident. Cartoonist Charles Schultz and the animators had to be intentional about Linus dropping his blanket at that particular moment. Soroski wrote, "The birth of Jesus separates us from our fears."[11]

And so it was with the paralytic man and his mat.

Put yourself in his shoes. If that was the only thing you owned besides the clothes on your back, that ratty old mat might be your security blanket. Your comfort mat.

And Jesus said to him, "Pick up your mat."

What? Wait! No, Jesus! I need that mat!

"Pick up your mat."

Jesus, it's been with me all my life, and, well, if this whole healing thing doesn't work out, I need it to sleep on, to comfort me.

But Jesus was saying to him, "You don't need that mat any longer. I'm about to work a miracle in your life, so you need to roll up that mat and put it away for good, because you'll never use it again. I'm taking you to a new destiny. I'm giving you a new plan and a new purpose, and you'll never need that old comfort mat again."

That's what happened to the paralytic man beside the Bethesda pool.

Likewise, Jesus is telling you to pick up your mat. Take it, roll it up, and move into a new destiny. You don't need a security blanket where you're going.

So what is your comfort mat? Is it the comfort mat of money? Is it the comfort mat of material things? Is it the comfort mat of people's approval? Is it the comfort mat of pleasure? Is it the comfort mat of achievement and success? What security blanket, what comfort mat, are you holding on to?

When those things become your comfort mat, you start trusting in them rather than the Miracle Worker, and you miss out on the miracle.

The Miracle Map suggests we look into the Bible's account of a miracle to see what it reveals about us, about our character. And I think we see much about ourselves in this miracle. We have to choose between our comfort mat and the miracle Jesus has for us.

It's sad, and telling, that so often we choose the mat.

C. S. Lewis put it this way: "We are half-hearted creatures, fooling about with drink and sex and ambition when infinite joy is offered us, like an ignorant child who wants to go on making mud pies in a slum because he cannot imagine what is meant by the offer of a holiday at the sea. We are far too easily pleased."[12]

We prefer the mud over the sea. We choose the ratty mat we've been living with rather than the redeeming miracle God has for us.

Ephesians 3:20 says, "Now glory be to God, who by his mighty power at work within us is able to do far more than we would ever dare to ask or even dream of—infinitely beyond our highest prayers, desires, thoughts, or hopes" (TLB). Did you catch that phrase "dare to ask or even dream of"? Can you dare to ask for or even dream of something beyond? God is saying to you, "I want to give you a miracle that's beyond anything you could ever imagine. But you have to get out of the mud puddle. You have to get up off the mat. You need to trust Me that there's so much more."

AND WALK

I'm to stand up and stop making excuses. I'm to let go of my comfort zone and grab the miracle zone. And then I have to start walking.

There is so much embedded in the last phrase of Jesus's words to the paralytic man. Just two words—"and walk"—yet they mean so much.

They might have been the scariest words this man had ever heard.

Walk? What if I fall and hurt myself?

Walk? What if I find that there is no miracle after all?

Walk? What if I realize, Jesus, that You're really not a miracle worker?

Walk? What if it works? What will I do? What will my life become?

Is the miracle you seek also a miracle you fear? Are you prepared to make the life change that a miracle brings? Are you willing *to walk*?

I like 1 John 4:18 as it is rendered in The Message: "Since fear is crippling, a fearful life—fear of death, fear of judgment—is one not yet fully formed in love."

Notice the choice of words here: "Since fear is crippling . . ." In so many ways the thing that paralyzes us in life is fear itself. We're afraid of so many things, aren't we? We fear what will happen when we no longer control our lives—even if our control right now is only over mud pies and ratty mats. We fear what might happen if we actually could live life fully and freely. We fear what it might mean to leave behind our comfort zones. We fear what it might mean to get unstuck and really *walk* into life.

As you look to find your miracle, you might do well to ask yourself the simple question "What am I afraid of?"

I think of this verse in Ephesians: "Therefore be imitators of God, as beloved children; and walk in love, just as Christ also loved you and gave Himself up for us" (5:1–2, NASB).

Walk in love.

And the apostle John wrote, "There is no room in love for fear. Well-formed love banishes fear" (1 John 4:18, MSG).

Love banishes fear.

We don't know what prompted the paralyzed man that day to stand up, take up his mat, and start walking. No doubt he felt fear and apprehension about what could go wrong. But something compelled him to do what Jesus commanded. I have to think he saw the love in Jesus's eyes, love that drove fear out of his mind and heart. And he walked.

We, too, need to focus on the loving eyes of Jesus. He is inviting you and me into a miracle. An amazing, life-changing, transforming, and scary miracle.

Trust in His love. Let His love drive out your fear.

A MIRACLE WE LEAST EXPECT

Finally, one Miracle Map principle is that God does the miracle His way, and it's often in a way you don't expect. You're sitting by the edge of the pool and looking for assistance, for healing, for an escape from your circumstances. Then Jesus does something you never thought or even imagined He'd do.

And so it was with the paralytic. This Bethesda pool and the healing waters must have seemed like a cruel game to him. It must have felt like torture—as if his lifelong paralysis weren't enough—that when the waters occasionally moved, no one was ever there to pick him up and place him in the pool. If only . . . just one time . . . this could happen.

Jesus asked him, "Would you like to get well?"

And the paralytic man said to Jesus, "I can't, sir, for I have no one to put me into the pool when the water bubbles up. Someone else always gets there ahead of me."

His words suggest both hopelessness and hope. His voice descends into the depths of self-pity and then rises in anticipation of what this Jesus might do for him, as if to say, "Have pity on me, Sir, please. Maybe You're the One who can help me get into the water."

Clearly he saw his deliverance and healing in the waters of the Bethesda pool.

Instead, Jesus, the Son of the God of All Surprises, said to him, "Stand up, pick up your mat, and walk!"

No healing pool needed. No magic. No troubled waters.

Jesus was saying to the paralytic, "Don't look over there at the pool. That won't save you. The miracle is over here. Here I am."

And perhaps that's what Jesus is saying to you and me: "You think you need that kind of a miracle, but I have something else for you. You think you need this change or solution in your life, but I have a better idea. You think that will transform your life. But actually I will."

So often we're looking for the wrong miracle. We're looking at the pool of troubled waters when we have the source of living water.

Jesus Himself.

Promises for When You're Stuck

Hear my cry, O God;
    listen to my prayer.

From the ends of the earth I call to you,
    I call as my heart grows faint;
    lead me to the rock that is higher than I.

Psalm 61:1–2

Walk in the way of love, just as Christ loved us and gave himself
up for us as a fragrant offering and sacrifice to God.

Ephesians 5:2

I can do all this through him who gives me strength.

Philippians 4:13

Trust God from the bottom of your heart;
    don't try to figure out everything on your own.
Listen for God's voice in everything you do, everywhere you go;
    he's the one who will keep you on track.
Don't assume that you know it all.
    Run to God! Run from evil!
Your body will glow with health,
    your very bones will vibrate with life!
Honor God with everything you own;
    give him the first and the best.

Your barns will burst,
    your wine vats will brim over.
But don't, dear friend, resent God's discipline;
    don't sulk under his loving correction.
It's the child he loves that God corrects;
    a father's delight is behind all this.

Proverbs 3:5–12, MSG

I know what it is to be in need, and I know what it is to have plenty. I have learned the secret of being content in any and every situation, whether well fed or hungry, whether living in plenty or in want.

Philippians 4:12

5

When You're Desperate

Jesus Heals a Woman with Internal Bleeding

A large crowd followed and pressed around him. And a woman was there who had been subject to bleeding for twelve years. She had suffered a great deal under the care of many doctors and had spent all she had, yet instead of getting better she grew worse. When she heard about Jesus, she came up behind him in the crowd and touched his cloak, because she thought, "If I just touch his clothes, I will be healed." Immediately her bleeding stopped and she felt in her body that she was freed from her suffering.

At once Jesus realized that power had gone out from him. He turned around in the crowd and asked, "Who touched my clothes?"

"You see the people crowding against you," his disciples answered, "and yet you can ask, 'Who touched me?'"

But Jesus kept looking around to see who had done it. Then the woman, knowing what had happened to her, came and fell at his feet and, trembling with fear, told him the whole truth. He said to her, "Daughter, your faith has healed you. Go in peace and be freed from your suffering."

—Mark 5:24–34

DEATH VALLEY, situated on the eastern edge of central California, is the lowest point in the United States. This massive landscape of sand and salt sits at 282 feet below sea level and stretches 140 miles long. Summer temperatures usually top 120 degrees, and Death Valley holds the record for the hottest temp ever recorded on earth—134 degrees Fahrenheit.

Visiting Death Valley in the summertime is not for the faint of heart. A friend of mine tells that when he was a kid, his family drove through the valley in early August. His parents' original idea was to camp there, but when they stopped at a one-pump gas station, the old geezer running the place simply pointed out at the desert sand extending miles into a wavy horizon and said, "Sure, you can camp here. Go ahead and pitch your tent anywhere." Hoping for a campground with at least one amenity in the form of a toilet, my friend's family decided to drive on and stay at a hotel on the other side.

But the drive was long, the temps were scorching, and the car eventually overheated. The dad decided to stop and let the radiator cool down, but he soon realized that "cool down" is a relative term in the heat of Death Valley. He tried to drive some more with the heater on in an attempt to draw the heat away from the engine. But that didn't help the radiator much, and it nearly gave the family a heat stroke. When they finally stopped on the side of the road with a radiator hissing and spitting boiling water, this family was scared. There was no traffic passing by, no known rest stops along the way, and not much hope they'd find help. Fortunately, help did arrive eventually, and they survived.

Does that feel familiar? Have you experienced your own death valley? A place where the heart and soul are dry and barren? A season that seems to go on forever without relief? A time when you've broken down on the side of the road? A low point in life that feels hopeless?

Maybe you're in such a situation now. Maybe you're so desperate you don't even know how to pray. You're painfully aware that you're in a desolate valley, but you don't know what to do to get out.

I can relate. I've been there too. At times I've been hurt so deeply or have had such a great need that I simply didn't have the words to pray. If you're like me, at those times you try to think through possible scenarios, searching for a decent solution, but each one leads to a dead end.

It's unspeakably comforting to me in the darkest times to know that we have a God who understands and a Helper who speaks for us when we have no words. Romans 8:26 tells us that "the Spirit helps us in our weakness. We do not know what we ought to pray for, but the Spirit himself intercedes for us through wordless groans."

God is waiting to meet your deepest needs just as He did for a woman who lived two thousand years ago. I think you'll see that her problems and the ultimate solution are the same for us today. We have a God we can reach out to when we're in a valley of desperation.

This woman was truly desperate. For twelve long years she had been suffering from an illness, going from doctor to doctor to doctor in hopes of finding relief. At this point her condition was worse, and she was broke.

How do you think this woman felt as she approached the crowd surrounding Jesus that day? We know that she'd been labeled incurable and that she was destitute, but her pain went far deeper. As a result of her sickness, she had the equivalent of a nonstop menstrual period. Under Jewish law a woman who was bleeding was considered unclean. Everyone and everything she touched became ceremonially unclean, so this woman would have been ostracized by the entire community, including her family. She couldn't even worship in the synagogue!

Can you imagine what it would be like not to have felt the touch of another human being for twelve years? This woman's physical problems had created social, emotional, and financial crises. Finally she was so desperate that she did something radical, even dangerous.

Personal Touch

This woman had heard about a man named Jesus, and the crowd was buzzing with accounts of how Jesus had just healed a demon-possessed man. She also had heard that a synagogue official named Jairus had asked Jesus to heal his dying daughter. That explained why the crowd following this miracle-worker Jesus was pressed in close.

But in the crowd was one place this woman wasn't supposed to be. However, desperate times call for desperate measures, so she waded into the crowd, despite her condition, despite the danger of being discovered.

Suddenly she knew what she had to do. She dared to believe that if she could simply reach out to Him and touch even the edge of His clothes, she'd be healed.

Scraping together every last bit of hope and courage and shoving aside her fear and shame, she stepped into the throng. I imagine her tucking her chin and pulling her cloak close to her face to avoid being recognized. She pushed her way through the crowd, likely overwhelmed by the physical contact after years of not being touched at all. Finally she made it to the front of the crowd and right behind Jesus.

In an act of scandalous faith, this woman reached out and, without saying a word, touched the hem of His cloak.

And instantly she was healed.

But the story doesn't end there with her experiencing the healing power of Jesus and the bliss of being pain-free for the first time in twelve years. She didn't fade back into the crowd without being discovered. No, that wasn't the end of it.

Her heart must have nearly stopped when Jesus suddenly turned around and said, "Who touched my clothes?"

His disciples basically answered, "Is that a joke, Jesus? I mean, people are crowding around You on all sides. How can You possibly ask, 'Who touched Me?'"

The crowd and even the disciples didn't realize that a miracle had taken place in their midst. Only Jesus and the woman knew.

What an incredible God! Without any fanfare or even a word being spoken, He knows and responds when one of His children reaches out to Him in faith.

Even though her bleeding had stopped, this woman still would have been considered unclean until she had undergone the usual elaborate postmenstrual washing ritual prescribed by Jewish law. But after she was healed, Jesus immediately called for the woman as if to say, "There is never a time when you cannot approach Me. You can never be too unclean for Me."

Is there an area of your life where you feel unclean? Have you been too ashamed even to put your prayer into words? Maybe you even feel unworthy of a miracle. Jesus already knows your need. Psalm 139:4 tells us: "Before a word is on my tongue you, LORD, know it completely." He already knows our deepest need. Our part is to reach out to Him in faith.

I don't know about you, but sometimes when I read a Bible story, I can get caught up in the cultural differences between first-century Jewish life and twenty-first-century Western-world life. For instance, in this story I could think, *They ostracized that woman for a bodily issue that she had no control over. That's crazy!* And it is. But it is no less crazy than the body shaming that's experienced by millions of women every single day. In fact, much of this ancient woman's story is painfully modern. Let's look at the comparisons:

High medical costs? *Check.*

Crowd mentality? *Check.*

Fear? Suffering? Shame? *Check, check, and check.*

The details might look different, but our problems are the same. And so is the answer.

Reach out to Jesus. Don't settle for anything less than personally touching Him. The same peace and freedom He gave to the woman in our story is available to you today.

Maybe you've tried everything you can think of to fix your problems but nothing has worked. You've used up all your money, all your energy, all your hope, and all your words. You're desperate. A wise theologian, Handley Moule, observed, "There is no situation so chaotic that God cannot, from that situation, create something that is surpassingly good. He did it at the creation. He did it at the cross. He is doing it today."[13]

THE MIRACLE AT THE END OF THE ROPE

Over and over again in Scripture we see people who had lived a long time with a great personal need and then were touched by Jesus. We see this in the Gospels. A man was blind from birth. The man at the Bethesda pool was paralyzed for thirty-eight years. The Samaritan woman at the well had, as Jesus pointed out, not one but five husbands. So often Jesus comes to us at the point we've practically given up hope.

A young woman from Wichita, Kansas, by the name of Kenya, tells the story of a sister she never knew. When Kenya was two years old, her mother gave birth to another daughter and gave her up for adoption.

After graduating from college in 2006, Kenya searched for her. "I simply prayed to God that if it was meant to be, it will be."

In 2011, Kenya and her sister were reunited. "It is almost as if God said, 'Give it to Me, and watch Me work.'"[14]

I know many people have prayed for miracles for years and years, and nothing happened. I don't wish in any way to diminish the agony and pain of that. I also don't want to suggest that God will always show up at the last moment like the cavalry riding in. But I do believe that as we look at and live in the miracles of Jesus, we will often see this truth from the Miracle Map applies: He catches us when we are at the end of our ropes. God grabs us when we let go. He says, *Give it to Me, and watch Me work.*

One of the most painful things to admit is that I need healing, that I really need God to do a work in my life that I can't do on my own. "God, I can't fix this relationship. You're going to have to do that." "God, I can't heal myself of this sickness. I need You to heal me." "God, I can't meet this need in my life. I need your help." It's humbling to pray such prayers! Yet the only people who receive healing are those who admit that they need healing.

This reminds me of the guy who was driving down the road and had a collision with a car that was towing a horse trailer. Months later the guy tried to claim damages for all his injuries, and the insurance company lawyer called him to dispute his claim. He said, "Why now, months after the accident, are you saying you were badly injured, when on the night of the accident, you said you were okay?" The man said, "Well, it was like this. I was lying in the road in agony. Then I heard someone say, 'The horse over there has a broken leg, and it looks like he's in a lot of pain.' The next thing I knew the policeman pulled out his gun and shot the horse. Then he came over to me and asked, 'Are you okay?' I emphatically said, 'Yes, I'm okay!' I was afraid of what would happen if I admitted my pain!"

Many times we tell people that we are okay. We're smiling on the outside, but on the inside we're aching and afraid. Let me tell you something about every person you're going to run into tomorrow—the people at your workplace, at your office, at your school, in your church, or in your neighborhood. I don't know them, and I don't know what they're going through. But let me tell you this: they're hurting. Everybody has a hidden hurt. Everybody needs healing.

And guess what? The people who are hurting the most are the people who will hurt you. Hurt people hurt people. When someone hurts you, remember it's because they are hurting deep down inside. That doesn't excuse them. I'm just saying we need to realize that everybody has a hidden hurt, and it will help you look at people in a different light.

GOD STILL HEALS

There are four ways God heals.

First, He can bring about physical healing. I believe with all my heart that God still heals physically. Because we see weird, extreme things like televangelists saying that if we send in a hundred dollars, we'll be healed, I think we go the opposite direction and don't pray for healing. God wants to heal today, yet many times we don't experience physical healing because we don't ask God to heal us or we don't believe that He is able to.

I also believe God often uses doctors and other medical professionals in the healing process. Many amazing Christian physicians pray before they perform surgery or treat a patient. But I believe God also uses medical professionals who are unbelievers, just as He used kings and leaders in the Bible who weren't believers, to fulfill His purposes.

Remember the Miracle Map. God will do the miracle in His way and in His time. He will use whomever He wants, however He wants, to accomplish His purpose.

In addition to physical healing, God gives emotional healing. Many people need emotional healing and don't even know it because we try to cover up our emotional pain. We're always busy. We're always around people. We always have noise on, like the radio or the television, or we're surfing the Internet or texting or posting. But in those quiet moments when we lay our heads on our pillows at night, we realize that we're empty on the inside, and the pain comes flooding into our lives. Don't run from those moments of pain. Run to God. Turn to Him. It's in our brokenness that God brings about His blessing.

Not only is God the source of physical and emotional healing, but He also brings relational healing. The landscape is littered with fragments of broken relationships. The sad thing about a shattered relationship is that the collateral damage is broken dreams and broken hearts. Maybe you need healing because you've been hurt in a relationship. If you're experiencing this kind of devastating pain, you need to know that God has the power to heal relationships and that He wants to heal your wounded heart.

The greatest miracle, however, is spiritual healing. It's the most important healing because our sins separate us from our holy and perfect God. Many of the hurts we have in our lives we bring on ourselves through our sins, mistakes, and failures. But the good news is that when we admit we need spiritual healing, God heals us. Look at David's words in Psalm 51:17: "My sacrifice, O God, is a broken spirit; a broken and contrite heart you, God, will not despise." When we're proud, God can't use us. But when we are broken, God can bless us. He can fill us with His strength and use us. If you are hurting today, God says at this moment, "I'll meet you right where you are. Bring your broken heart to Me." Remember the first principle of the Miracle Map: *God always starts with the miracle you need most.*

When we're broken and hurting, we realize we need God. Otherwise we think we can do life on our own. If I never had a problem, I would never get on my knees. Only when I feel the full weight of my problem will I go to Christ and request the miracle I need most.

One of the reasons God allows us to know desolate valleys and desperate times is so we'll depend on Him and live in close relationship with Him.

A DEEPER MIRACLE

Our desperation is what drives us to the source of miracles. But remember the second principle of the Miracle Map: *The miracle you need most leads you to what you really need most, a deeper relationship with God.*

I (Chris) wrote a book with our daughter, Megan, called *Beauty Begins.* It's about how girls and women can realize their true worth and beauty by discovering their sacred reflection in Christ's eyes. In the chapter "The Beauty of Brokenness," Megan described the valley of depression she went through in college, a valley that led her to what she needed most—a deeper relationship with God. Here's what she said:

It is never easy to deal with depression or any event or situation that makes you feel an overwhelming amount of despair and loneliness. I (Megan) have experienced those feelings of utter desolation and hopelessness, believing there was no point to life, no reason for living, and having no feelings but sadness and worthlessness. I have been in the worst place imaginable. All I wanted to do was sit in my room and cry or, better, just sleep for hours since it was the closest thing to not being alive.

In high school I was known as a very happy and energetic girl. People would ask me if I ever stopped smiling. I loved being funny and cheering people up. Honestly, it was difficult for me not to smile and be happy. It's who God had made me to be. I wondered how people could want to hurt or kill themselves. It didn't make sense to me. There is always something to live for, and I could not fathom the possibility of being so low and defeated that I felt like dying or taking my own life.

I couldn't understand until I felt that way myself. My freshman year of college I was hit with an uncontrollable wave of despair. I found myself believing there was no meaning to life and being so sad and upset and in such pain that I felt nothing would make me happier than to go on to heaven. In a way I was right. We are meant for heaven, and nothing on this earth is going to totally satisfy us. But we are also meant to live satisfying and fulfilling lives while here on earth!

People had told me that college would be the best four years of my life. Though some of my best memories come from my college days, I can also say that those four years were the most difficult of my life. I had absolutely loved high school. I was a cheerleader, had amazing friends, made good grades, was involved at church, and had everything going for me—except I wasn't very close to the Lord.

That first year of college I had only a couple of friends. I wasn't involved in anything. My family was three hours away. I didn't know how to study. I was discouraged and terribly lonely. These factors, along with a genetic tendency, combined to create the perfect storm of clinical depression.

In a big way I'm grateful I've had to deal with depression, because it has taught me to depend on God! And being the selfish person I am, I needed that. I needed God to kick the pedestal out from under me so I would realize that life isn't all about me and that I actually do need Him. During the most difficult time, I would wake up every morning with my eyes wide open to God and say, "Lord, I definitely cannot get through this day without You. Please help me follow You today, and bring me joy through this difficult time." I *had* to read my Bible every day. I *had* to pray continually. I *had* to grow closer to God. Man, I hated the loneliness and pain. But, wow, did I love growing closer to God! I grew so close to God through that time. Life began to have meaning and importance again, and I started to find joy in the little things. I finally turned my attention from myself to God and started letting Him love other people through me.

God has taken my depression and used it—more than anything else in my life—to deepen my faith. That's the beauty of brokenness. God has used my pain and problems to bring me to the end of myself so I would depend totally on Him. He has also taught me that I need to humbly accept the help of others, including a Christian doctor whom God has used greatly in my continued healing. Beauty begins where self-reliance ends.[15]

We have a God who heals. He cares about you as you walk through a valley. But as Megan discovered, the deeper miracle He wants to do in your life is to draw you closer to Himself so you'll discover the whole reason He created you. And that is to be in a deep and lasting love relationship with the Source of all miracles.

Let's look at a heart miracle that Jesus did for another woman who needed spiritual healing. It's a familiar story—Jesus's encounter with the Samaritan woman at the well. It's not included in the usual lists of Jesus's miracles. Jesus didn't walk on water or calm a storm. He didn't heal anyone.

Or did He?

As you may recall, Jesus was passing through Samaria when He stopped at a well. There He asked a Samaritan woman for a drink.

The Bible informs us that the disciples had gone into town for food, so we have the rare situation of Jesus being alone. It feels like a play—Jesus and this woman talking together—and it unfolds like drama with riveting dialogue.

> Jesus said to her, "Will you give me a drink?" (His disciples had gone into the town to buy food.)
>
> The Samaritan woman said to him, "You are a Jew and I am a Samaritan woman. How can you ask me for a drink?" (For Jews do not associate with Samaritans.)
>
> Jesus answered her, "If you knew the gift of God and who it is that asks you for a drink, you would have asked him and he would have given you living water."
>
> "Sir," the woman said, "you have nothing to draw with and the well is deep. Where can you get this living water? Are you greater than our father Jacob, who gave us the well and drank from it himself, as did also his sons and his livestock?" (John 4:7–12)

It's fascinating, this back-and-forth discussion of physical and spiritual water. Jesus is the great Aha! of life, isn't He? Here He is alone with a woman.

His being a Jew and her being a Samaritan isn't lost on her. While she has known, as we shall see, many other men, this man is different. Aha! has walked into her life.

He talked about living water, and she asked to know more:

> Jesus answered, "Everyone who drinks this water will be thirsty again, but whoever drinks the water I give them will never thirst. Indeed, the water I give them will become in them a spring of water welling up to eternal life."
>
> The woman said to him, "Sir, give me this water so that I won't get thirsty and have to keep coming here to draw water." (verses 13–15)

It's interesting that the Bible's miracle stories often start with someone coming to Jesus and stating their problem. "There's this guy, see, and he's crippled" or "My daughter is dying" or "Jesus, the storm is going to capsize the boat!" But here the encounter started with the solution. With living water. With Jesus Himself. However, a bit later the problem emerged when Jesus told the woman to get her husband. Of course, He already knew her situation.

> "I have no husband," she replied.
>
> Jesus said to her, "You are right when you say you have no husband. The fact is, you have had five husbands, and the man you now have is not your husband. What you have just said is quite true."
>
> "Sir," the woman said, "I can see that you are a prophet. Our ancestors worshiped on this mountain, but you Jews claim that the place where we must worship is in Jerusalem." (verses 17–20)

The Samaritan woman must have been stunned. Jesus, the Great Aha!, had peered into her life, and He knew exactly what her problem was, what her need was, what her sickness was. She wasn't blind or crippled or paralyzed physically, but maybe she was emotionally. Or maybe relationally she was just as paralyzed as the man at the Bethesda pool.

Like many recipients of miracles in the Gospels, the Samaritan woman acknowledged who Jesus was:

> The woman said, "I know that Messiah" (called Christ) "is coming.
> When he comes, he will explain everything to us."
>   Then Jesus declared, "I, the one speaking to you—I am he."
> (verses 25–26)

The woman named the man who was to come: the Messiah. The Christ. She didn't have to say much more. She was really asking, "Are you this man?" And the ongoing subtext is clear: "If You are this man, I need to have what You are offering. I need this Living Water. I need You."

And of course, Jesus replied, "I am he" (verse 26).

Later in the passage we read:

> Many of the Samaritans from that town believed in him because of
> the woman's testimony, "He told me everything I ever did." (verse 39)

What happened here was a miracle. It wasn't a physical miracle that we normally count among the thirty-some miracles Jesus performed on earth. But it was a heart miracle. He transformed the Samaritan woman's heart.

And we need to remember this so we don't miss the point: God's work in people often starts with a physical miracle but always yields a heart miracle as well. We should never allow our eagerness to see and experience physical miracles blind us to the possibility and reality of the heart miracles that occur around us all the time.

The Power of the Cross

One of the greatest promises on healing in the Bible is Isaiah 53:5: "But he was pierced for our transgressions, he was crushed for our iniquities; the punishment that brought us peace was on him, and by his wounds we are healed."

Christ died on the cross to heal us from our hurts, from our sins, from our sicknesses, from our wounds. The Healer is familiar with your wounds, and He has the power to heal you. Like the woman in our story, you just have to reach out to Him in faith.

Always remember, however, the third principle of the Miracle Map: *God does the miracle in His time and in His way.*

When we're hurting and going through the valley of desperation, we often expect God's healing to conform to our timetable. Sometimes God does heal immediately, at the moment we reach out to Him in prayer. Over and over again in our church, we've seen God work miracles immediately, so we pray expectantly and with great faith!

When the church was just a couple of years old, we ran out of space in the small elementary school where we had been holding Sunday worship services. God had grown us, and we needed a bigger place to meet. I thought it was really fortunate that a new and very large high school had just been built in our area on fifty acres of land that included lots of parking spaces.

I took several of our church leaders to meet with leaders of the school district to inquire about holding our Sunday church services at the new high school. I explained to the school administrators that we were now a large church—with influential people in the community as members—and that we really needed to lease the new high school on Sundays.

They quickly gave their answer: no. They explained that even though they appreciated our church for what it did in the community, the school board had voted that no church would ever be allowed to rent the high school on Sundays.

They graciously offered any of the elementary schools, but they were all too small for our church.

We didn't give up easily, but after several more fruitless meetings and conversations, we found ourselves at a dead end. I'll never forget driving by the new high school after one of those meetings when we were told that no church would ever meet in the high school. I prayed and poured my heart out. I said, *God, I don't understand. I thought for sure You wanted us to have room for all the people who want to come to our church and find a relationship with You. Why aren't You opening the doors of the new high school for us?*

It was one of those times when God spoke so clearly to my heart that there was no mistaking it. *I want to open up the doors of the high school to My church, but you haven't trusted Me. You've been acting like the church is big enough now that you don't need Me.*

God then impressed upon me to gather our small staff, walk around the high school, and pray for the walls that were keeping us from leasing the school to come down.

At first I tried to dismiss what God was saying. I thought, *Lord, You don't really want us to do that, do You? I'm sure that's just a crazy idea that popped in my head because I've been reading the book of Joshua in my quiet time. That can't be from You, can it?*

But deep down I knew the plan was His. So I immediately told our staff to meet me in the morning, and we were going to walk around the high school and pray. We all arrived early the next morning even though we weren't exactly sure how this would go. But we started walking around the school property, all fifty acres, praying for the walls to come down.

We sang and prayed for God to make a way where there seemed to be no way. After walking around the school a couple of times, we left the school property and left the miracle in God's hands.

As soon as I got home, my phone rang. It was the county commissioner who was a member of our church. He said, "I just got off the phone with the superintendent of schools, and he's had a change of heart. He's given us a green light to lease the high school on Sundays."

I told him, "You won't believe what we just did!" After I told him about our march around the school, he said, "That gives me chills. I was calling the superintendent but thinking, *Why am I trying yet another time?*" He went on to say, "Now I know!"

At times we've prayed in faith and God has given us a miracle instantly, as with the use of the new high school. There have been many times, however, when we've prayed for a miracle, and it's been several weeks, months, or years before the miracle arrived. We prayed for eight years before we were able to move into our own church building, but God strengthened us and provided many miracles along the way.

When it comes to healing, sometimes we don't see the answer to our prayers right away. Instead, there is delayed healing. Sometimes God takes us through a healing process. I'm not going to lie; it can be painful as we wait for healing. When I go through that painful healing process, He smoothes the rough edges of my character that don't look like Christ. Sometimes He changes the circumstances in my life, and sometimes He changes me in those circumstances. If you're waiting for healing in your life right now, don't give up. Keep praying. Just know that while you're going through this delay, God is still fulfilling His purpose in your life because He's more interested in your character than your comfort.

Understand that the pain you are going through can't derail God's purpose for your life.

A View from the Top

Death Valley is the lowest point in North America, yet it's very close to the highest summit in the United States.

Just eighty-four miles away from Death Valley, Mount Whitney stands tall, rising to some 14,500 feet above sea level. From its summit one can look across the great expanse that is Death Valley. It's an awesome view. From that perspective Death Valley is small and far away. The heat and barren wasteland that one experiences when journeying through Death Valley is a beautiful landscape when viewed from the summit of Mount Whitney.

The Cross of Christ is the Mount Whitney to our Death Valley.

From the perspective of the Cross, the valley we find ourselves in is small and distant, conquered by the sheer height of the immensity of what God is doing in our lives. From the perspective of the Cross, our valley takes on new meaning, for the Cross itself was a valley like no other.

And we need to remember that the Miracle Worker who has already climbed that mountain can certainly lift us out of the valley.

We're not in heaven yet. There is pain on this earth. There is hurt on this earth. There is sickness on this earth. Even if you receive a healing miracle—I'm sorry to break this to you—you will eventually die. The last time I checked, the mortality rate was 100 percent.

But here's the good news. As believers, we have a place called heaven where we'll experience ultimate healing. It's a perfect place with no more sickness, no more sorrow, no more pain, no more death, no more disease. Some have said, "In heaven don't you just sit up there on a cloud and play a harp?" Nope. Heaven's not like that. Heaven is the most fulfilling place you could ever imagine, and heaven is waiting for us.

People sometimes ask me, "Why doesn't God heal everyone? Do they lack faith?" No, I don't believe that. I've seen people with great faith who prayed for physical healing, and God didn't heal them. He took them on to heaven. I don't understand why God doesn't heal everyone immediately, but I know this with all my heart: there is a place called heaven where one day we'll all experience ultimate healing.

Promises for When You Feel Desperate

You are my hiding place;

you will protect me from trouble

and surround me with songs of deliverance.

Psalm 32:7

Trust in the LORD with all your heart

and lean not on your own understanding;

in all your ways submit to him,

and he will make your paths straight.

Proverbs 3:5–6

Call on me in the day of trouble;

I will deliver you, and you will honor me.

Psalm 50:15

Jesus said, "Come to me, all of you who are weary and carry heavy burdens, and I will give you rest."

Matthew 11:28, NLT

Moreover we know that to those who love God, who are called according to his plan, everything that happens fits into a pattern for good.

Romans 8:28, Phillips

Jesus: The Provider

A miracle is when the whole is greater than the sum of its parts. A miracle is when one plus one equals a thousand.

—Frederick Buechner

The will of God will never take us where the grace of God cannot sustain us.

—Billy Graham

6

When You're Overwhelmed

Jesus Feeds the Five Thousand

Some time after this, Jesus crossed to the far shore of the Sea of Galilee (that is, the Sea of Tiberias), and a great crowd of people followed him because they saw the signs he had performed by healing the sick. Then Jesus went up on a mountainside and sat down with his disciples. The Jewish Passover Festival was near.

When Jesus looked up and saw a great crowd coming toward him, he said to Philip, "Where shall we buy bread for these people to eat?" He asked this only to test him, for he already had in mind what he was going to do.

Philip answered him, "It would take more than half a year's wages to buy enough bread for each one to have a bite!"

Another of his disciples, Andrew, Simon Peter's brother, spoke up, "Here is a boy with five small barley loaves and two small fish, but how far will they go among so many?"

Jesus said, "Have the people sit down." There was

plenty of grass in that place, and they sat down (about five
thousand men were there). Jesus then took the loaves, gave
thanks, and distributed to those who were seated as much
as they wanted. He did the same with the fish.

When they had all had enough to eat, he said to his
disciples, "Gather the pieces that are left over. Let nothing
be wasted." So they gathered them and filled twelve baskets
with the pieces of the five barley loaves left over by those
who had eaten.

—John 6:1–13

MORE THAN TWO DECADES AGO a business book was written that changed
the way corporate America thinks. It was written by Jim Collins and titled
Built to Last. The core purpose of the book was to look at America's top companies and figure out what made them successful.

In *Built to Last* one key idea emerged. It was an element common to many
of the companies that were evaluated, and it had to do with the primary goal a
company established for itself.

Collins labeled this the "Big Hairy Audacious Goal." Shortened to its ini-
tials, it was BHAG, pronounced "Bee-Hag." Collins claimed that successful
companies set for themselves a huge goal. Not an easy goal. Not a safe goal. Not
a modest goal. But a goal that was audacious. Something that made people gasp.
A BHAG.

One well-known BHAG was issued by John F. Kennedy in 1961: "I believe
that this nation should commit itself to achieving the goal, before this decade is
out, of landing a man on the moon and returning him safely to the earth. No
single space project in this period will be more impressive to mankind, or more

important for the long-range exploration of space."[16] It was an audacious goal. No one believed it could be done, much less within the decade.

One corporate example of a BHAG came from the Boeing Corporation in the midsixties. On the drawing board was the design of a massive super-jetliner, the 747. At the time nothing of that size had been built. The Boeing chairman famously set forth the company BHAG in 1965: "We will build it even if it takes the resources of the entire company." In other words, he was literally prepared to bet the company on the project.[17]

I imagine that some employees of a company hear their CEO, in a state-of-the-company address, present an ambitious new BHAG and simply think, *Oh brother, that's impossible* or *No way! Can't be done.* One person's BHAG is another person's obstacle—and one that seems impossible to overcome.

The miracle of the feeding of the five thousand occurred after Jesus had been teaching and preaching around the Sea of Galilee. As His ministry grew, so did the crowds following Him. In fact, Scripture indicates that Jesus and the disciples climbed into a boat and sailed a short way from the coast just to get away from the crowds for a time of rest. They disembarked on the shore, looking for some peace and quiet, only to see people running along the coast, following them.

It was late in the day, and this area was remote, meaning that these thousands of people would not be able to get home that night to eat. The question quickly became how to feed everyone.

I'm pretty sure that Jesus saw this situation as a BHAG. Meanwhile, His disciples saw it as an impossible problem. Both faced the same question: "How will we feed these people?" But their responses were vastly different.

I find it fascinating how Jesus spoke to His disciples here. He turned to Philip and asked, "Where shall we buy bread for these people to eat?" I can imagine Philip looking at Him as if Jesus were out of His mind. He might have said, "Really, Jesus? Like there's a grocery store in nearby Bethsaida? Yeah, so why don't Andrew and I just run down to the super and pick up some bread and fish for, say, five thousand people. You've got to be kidding me. I mean, it's not even a Costco!"

No, Philip didn't say that, but he did protest strongly: "It would take more than half a year's wages to buy enough bread for each one to have a bite!" Philip was saying to Jesus, "This is an impossible goal. You don't know what you're asking!"

Of course Jesus knew *exactly* what He was asking.

And we'd do well to pay attention.

Jesus was actually pointing Philip and the disciples to how big and hairy and audacious the goal in front of them was. To underscore the audaciousness of the task, He was suggesting that *they* do it. "How are you going to feed these people?" He asked. "How are you going to pay for it?" Jesus wanted them to acknowledge the impossible mountain in front of them. "How will you accomplish this?"

I don't think it was a taunt. Jesus wasn't egging them on. He was teaching them a lesson. Jesus was stretching the faith of Philip and the other disciples.

To me, the surprise here isn't that the disciples couldn't figure out how they could feed everyone. The surprise is they didn't imagine that Jesus could. You would think one of the more insightful disciples might have gotten it and said to Jesus, "Well, Rabbi, we kind of, uh, well, we were thinking that maybe You could do one of Your miracles here."

But that didn't happen. Somehow the disciples failed to expect Jesus to work a miracle here.

In the course of Jesus's ministry on earth, He performed around three dozen miracles that are recorded. This miracle of feeding the five thousand occurred in the middle of Jesus's ministry, so the disciples had already witnessed Jesus perform many miracles.

Yet here on this hillside overlooking the Sea of Galilee, they seemed clueless about what could possibly be done to feed thousands of hungry people. Maybe what they remembered was that Jesus's previous miracles had been mostly one-on-one encounters—healing a blind man here, casting out some demons there. Nothing on this scale. Perhaps, despite all the miracles the disciples had witnessed, they thought this vast sea of people stretching before them to the horizon was, even for this Miracle Worker, above His pay grade.

As Jesus tested Philip's faith, neither Philip nor the other disciples suggested that Jesus Himself perform a miracle. It was as if they didn't remember or understand what He'd done before.

Perhaps the reason they overlooked the Source of miracles who was right in front of them was that they were totally overwhelmed by the problem. Whenever I start feeling overwhelmed, it's easy to forget about everything else in my life except for the overwhelming problem in front of me.

There's definitely a spiritual memory loss that occurs when we feel overwhelmed. We forget about all the blessings in our lives, and we focus solely on the burdens. We forget about all the times in the past God came through just when we needed Him most. We forget how big and great God is, and we forget how much He cares about us.

Sometimes the best thing we can do when we're feeling overwhelmed is just to stop. Stop doing. Stop worrying. Just stop and be still. Our natural response when we feel as if we're drowning in an ocean of activity is to work harder, to get more frenzied, and to be busy doing. But there's a tremendous danger to working harder, not smarter. We get distracted, and then our work and our busyness become destructive. Many relationships are being destroyed today because we don't stop long enough to truly see how our overcrowded schedules and our frantic lifestyles are resulting in shallow and weak relationships.

The main thing we're forgetting, however, is that we're not God. We can't solve every problem, and we can't control the universe, not even the problem in front of us. Remember what God says to us in Psalm 46:10: "Be still, and know that I am God."

Remember, He's God. You're not! The great news is that, just like the disciples, we can turn to the Source of miracles, who can carry our burdens and do the impossible in our lives.

Andrew was the disciple who came at least a little closer to imagining the impossible miracle Jesus was about to perform. He said, "Well, there's a boy here with some barley loaves and fish." It's as if Andrew was halfway to understanding what might be possible. He seemed to have a seed of faith, but he still couldn't quite connect the dots.

Where do you see yourself in this story? What is your overwhelming situation? Are you a Philip saying it's impossible? Or are you an Andrew saying, "Well, maybe, just maybe"? Or by remembering the things He already has done, are you able to imagine that Jesus can take your impossible situation and work a miracle?

REMEMBER WHAT GOD CAN DO

We know from the context and the geography of the land around Galilee that this crowd of five thousand was Jewish. So these people would have known about another miracle that had occurred some fourteen hundred years earlier. That story was baked into their culture and faith.

Their ancestors, the Israelites, wandered in the wilderness after fleeing from the Egyptians. The people of Israel complained that there was no food, and they were hungry. They murmured that they would have been better off still working as slaves for the Egyptians. At least there in Egypt, so they said, they knew they would be fed. In response to the grumbling, the Lord appeared to Moses and said, "I will rain down bread from heaven for you" (Exodus 16:4). And so it happened that manna came down from heaven for all the Israelites day after day. The Bible says, "Everyone had gathered just as much as they needed" (verse 18).

It was a miracle. God provided bread for thousands of people.

It was no accident that Jesus and the disciples found themselves on the side of a mountain looking across a great expanse of people. (By the way, the Bible records specifically that the crowd numbered five thousand *men*. So likely there were many more present when the women and children were included.) It is also interesting that this occurred on the eve of Passover, the Jewish holiday commemorating the freeing of the Jews from ancient Egypt so long ago. A holiday also known as the Feast of the Unleavened Bread.

So in the presence of this massive Jewish crowd, it was no accident that this miracle was about to echo the famous miracle of the feeding of the Jewish people centuries before.

In fact, this is a picture of divine intention—the preparation of a huge stage for what was about to happen. It was God aligning time and people to land here in this place. It was the arrangement of circumstances that brought Jesus and His disciples before a multitude of thousands in order to achieve one grand, glorious, and most audacious goal.

This event was indeed staged by God Himself at the turning point of Jesus's ministry. After this, Jesus would no longer be a local secret. After this, He would be known throughout the region. And after this, people would talk about Him: "Did you hear what that man Jesus did? I was there. I remember what happened that day."

Do we? Do we remember? Do we remember what God has done, back then and now in our lives?

How can we absorb this incredible cosmic event on that hillside in Galilee, remember what God did then, and still doubt what He can do now, today?

This miracle isn't really just about Jesus providing for a bunch of people.

You might have heard of a reality TV show, a cooking show, called *Dinner: Impossible.* The host is Robert Irvine, a chef and fitness fanatic. (He must work out like crazy because he has upper arms the size of redwood tree trunks.) The concept of the show is to present Irvine and his team of cooks with impossible cooking challenges. Usually these involve large crowds at a conference or party and specialized food requirements to fit the theme of the occasion. Always the challenge is timed—just a certain number of hours before the food must be served. So we follow Irvine and his cooking disciples as they race the clock.

But Jesus's miracle wasn't like that. Jesus was not dealing with some last-minute menu to be cooked under stress, and the situation was not about catering trucks pulling up alongside the Galilean crowd. The event was really not about food at all. Not that kind of food.

This miracle was about provision. About remembering how God provides. How He provided manna from heaven before. How He can provide now. How, as we shall see, He will provide in the future.

This is not about *Dinner: Impossible*. It's about *Life: Possible*.

This feeding of the five thousand is the only miracle recorded in all four gospels. The story is the same each time, but the four writers include slightly different details. There's a short verse in Mark's account that is easy to miss: "When Jesus landed and saw a large crowd, he had compassion on them, because they were like sheep without a shepherd" (6:34).

The miracle was not just about material food. It was about Jesus, about God being present with those who need a shepherd. It was about Him providing for you and me. It was about Jesus standing on a hillside saying, "I am here, and we're going to do something amazing. Just like before. Remember?"

Do you remember what He's done before?

Are you looking for a miracle in your life? It might be big or small, but so often even the smallest needs feel huge and impossible.

If you are to find your miracle today, you need to remember what God has done in the past. How have you experienced God's provision in the past? I encourage you to spend time in prayer with God, not just asking Him for your miracle, but also recounting all the things He's done for you in the past.

I love this verse in Ephesians: "Now all glory to God, who is able, through his mighty power at work within us, to accomplish infinitely more than we might ask or think" (3:20, NLT). I suggest you put this on your refrigerator and memorize it.

This verse is saying that God wants to do more in your life than you can ever imagine, think, or dream. He has a plan for you, a BHAG, and He wants to achieve this audacious goal. The problems you face are part of God's plan to help you focus on what *He can do,* not on what *you can't do.*

Maybe you're saying, like Philip, "God, there's this big impossible situation in front of me right now. I can't do this. I'm totally overwhelmed."

And He is saying, "No, you can't do it. But I can."

Or maybe, like Andrew, you're saying, "God, I don't have much. Just these few loaves and fish."

If that's you, hear God reply, "I'll work with that. By the way, remember what I've done before?"

Whatever you are going through, I can tell you this: nothing is impossible for God. Remember what God can do.

START WITH SOMETHING SMALL

The miracle of the feeding of the five thousand is a vision of contrasts, the very big and the very small. Picture the movie version: the camera pans across the Sea of Galilee to the crowd, then glides across the thousands of people, row after row of men, women, and children, and then eventually swoops toward the hillside where Jesus and the disciples are standing. Then the camera stops, focuses, and zooms in on one small boy with an even smaller basket of bread and fish.

As Jesus and His disciples stood surveying this massive crowd, maybe He was making another point. In Mark's account the disciples suggested Jesus should send the crowd away to neighboring villages to get some dinner. Jesus replied instead, "You give them something to eat" (6:37).

I think Jesus was maybe saying to them, "Think again. Take a second look at this. What do we already have here?"

And this is when Andrew came forward and spoke about the little boy's lunch. "Here is a boy with five small barley loaves and two small fish, but how far will they go among so many?"

Remember the Miracle Map. God works the miracle His way.

There's a great lesson in this story for us today as we look to find a miracle in our lives. So often we're looking for the big miracle. We're seeing the size of the obstacle, the rows and rows of problems we're facing. We cry out, "I need something big here, God!"

God replies, "What do you have? Take a second look and bring Me whatever you have."

We look at Him. We're a little clueless like Philip was, and we say, "What? I really don't have much, Lord. What I have is so small."

Bingo. That's what God wants. The small thing we have.

God always starts with what we already have.

So why did Jesus use the loaves and fish that day?

Well, I could say something about the symbolism of the bread (we'll get to that later in this chapter), and I believe there's something beautiful about God using a small lunch from a small boy to feed a big multitude. But I think there's something more here. I think we might take a cue from the Miracle Map.

Another of the Miracle Map principles is that God starts with the miracle you think you need most, but He leads you to what you really need most, a deeper relationship with Christ. Miracles are transformational. And I think that God starts with what you have, the little thing you can give, because He wants to *involve you in the miracle*. He wants us to participate in the supernatural event He is working.

I don't know what happened to that boy that day, but I have to think he was amazed as he watched his picnic lunch being passed forward and then multiplied to feed thousands. I can't imagine any kid walking away from that experience without being transformed. Likewise, I don't know what will happen to you in the days to come, but I think that when God involves you in the miracle He is about to do, it will transform you in a powerful way.

God wants us to be a part of the work He does.

So He starts with what we have. The small thing we have. The thing we overlook until He says, "Think again. What do you have for Me?"

I think it's His way of saying, "Are you with Me in this? Or are you on the sidelines watching, a bystander?"

Again, I believe He can do miracles either way—with us or without us. But by giving Him even the little thing we have—our hushed prayer, a crumb of faith, a simple act of love—we participate in the work He is doing in our lives and in the lives of others. We align ourselves with His supernatural power, and we have a part in the miracle itself.

When God takes our overwhelming obstacle and does this amazing miracle, we are changed. When He takes the small thing we have and works wonders with it, we find ourselves transformed, and we grow closer to the Miracle Worker.

Often that's the more significant miracle.

THE RIPPLE EFFECT

There's another image here as well. One that gives me chills.

The image is of the church and God's people. The gospel of Mark reports the miracle this way:

> Taking the five loaves and the two fish and looking up to heaven, he
> gave thanks and broke the loaves. Then he gave them to his disciples
> to distribute to the people. He also divided the two fish among them
> all. They all ate and were satisfied, and the disciples picked up twelve
> basketfuls of broken pieces of bread and fish. (6:41–43)

Once again let's imagine the scene as if we were there. This is how I see it happening. Jesus is standing with the bread loaves and the fish, breaking the bread and handing it to each of His disciples, who pass it on to the first people sitting before them. Those people have more left over, which they pass on to others behind them. And those have more left over and do the same. Imagine that sunny hillside in Galilee. Watch as the people receive their food and turn, and see the ripple of humanity in a great wave as the food, ever multiplying, makes its way out to the people at the farthest edge of the horizon.

This is, of course, the story of the good news and our part in it. It is a picture of the spread of the gospel through time and history. It is a beautiful image of how we are part of the great miracle of redemption in human history.

God uses the ripple effect. Like a pebble in a pond, you and I are part of the work of God that goes forward, touches others, and transforms lives. We are part of the cascade of events that started with Jesus and His disciples, then the apostles and the early church, and down through time to the present day.

Likewise, the miracle God has for you might be the start of a ripple that will extend to others around you and into eternity.

But note that the miracle of the feeding of the five thousand started with the bread being broken: "He gave thanks and broke the loaves."

The miracle really starts here.

Before God can work with you and me, before the bread can be multiplied, we have to be broken. As you look to find your miracle, understand the power of being broken. Know that a miracle in your life will happen in the context of your realizing your own powerlessness, your brokenness, and remembering what God can do.

God has to allow you and me to be broken of our pride, of thinking we can handle the problem on our own, of believing we can somehow come up with a solution by ourselves.

Has He already been breaking you?

Maybe you've experienced a broken heart. Your emotions have been shattered. Your dreams have been shattered. Your life is in pieces emotionally.

Maybe your self-esteem has been shaken as your business has faltered, or you've lost your job, or you've been rejected too many times in your job search.

Maybe you've been broken physically, and after years of great health and strength, you're now feeling weak and vulnerable.

I believe with all my heart that God allows us to go through times of brokenness so He can bless us. Brokenness always precedes blessedness. Jesus broke the bread, and then He did the miracle. If you are at a place of brokenness right now, be ready. God is about to act.

"My Body, Broken"

Too often we read the miracle of the feeding of the five thousand and stop where the heading in our Bible stops. In fact, the miracle continues for ten more verses in the gospel of John.

There's more.

It was the day after the thousands were fed. The crowds were still buzzing from what they'd experienced. In fact, they couldn't get enough of Jesus and sought Him out on the side of the lake. The Bible says:

When they found him on the other side of the lake, they asked him, "Rabbi, when did you get here?"

Jesus answered, "Very truly I tell you, you are looking for me, not because you saw the signs I performed but because you ate the loaves and had your fill. Do not work for food that spoils, but for food that endures to eternal life, which the Son of Man will give you. For on him God the Father has placed his seal of approval."

Then they asked him, "What must we do to do the works God requires?"

Jesus answered, "The work of God is this: to believe in the one he has sent."

So they asked him, "What sign then will you give that we may see it and believe you? What will you do? Our ancestors ate the manna in the wilderness; as it is written: 'He gave them bread from heaven to eat.'"

Jesus said to them, "Very truly I tell you, it is not Moses who has given you the bread from heaven, but it is my Father who gives you the true bread from heaven. For the bread of God is the bread that comes down from heaven and gives life to the world."

"Sir," they said, "always give us this bread."

Then Jesus declared, "I am the bread of life. Whoever comes to me will never go hungry, and whoever believes in me will never be thirsty." (John 6:25–35)

Jesus waited until the next day to deliver the punch line. First, He said, essentially, "That miracle yesterday wasn't about what you think it was about. You are looking for Me because you got fed physically. But the real miracle is about eternal food and eternal life."

And soon Jesus says it: "I am the bread of life."

That is what the feeding of the five thousand is really about.

Suddenly other connections flood our minds. We remember another event in Jesus's life that the crowds back then wouldn't yet know of. Another meal Jesus shared with His disciples. The Last Supper.

At that later meal Jesus again took the bread and broke it, and He said, "This is my body, which is broken for you" (1 Corinthians 11:24, KJV).

We remember the scene on that hillside as the broken pieces of five loaves and two fish were passed along row after row, a ripple effect, extending further through time into the present. And we remember that it represents Jesus Himself, God, present with us.

We need to remember in our brokenness that Jesus was broken for us.

We need to remember in our search for a miracle—one that I believe God will provide to you and me—that ultimately Jesus, the bread of life, is the only real miracle we need.

Promises for When You're Overwhelmed

From the end of the earth I will cry to You,
When my heart is overwhelmed;
Lead me to the rock that is higher than I.

Psalm 61:2, NKJV

You are of God, little children, and have overcome them, because
He who is in you is greater than he who is in the world.

1 John 4:4, NKJV

He says, "Be still, and know that I am God;
I will be exalted among the nations,
I will be exalted in the earth."

Psalm 46:10

Jesus looked at them and said, "With man this is impossible,
but with God all things are possible."

Matthew 19:26

He refreshes my soul.
He guides me along the right paths
for his name's sake.

Psalm 23:3

Come to me, all you who are weary and burdened, and I will give
you rest.

Matthew 11:28

No, despite all these things, overwhelming victory is ours through Christ, who loved us.

Romans 8:37, NLT

7

When You're Discouraged

Jesus Fills the Empty Nets

One day as Jesus was standing by the Lake of Gennesaret, the people were crowding around him and listening to the word of God. He saw at the water's edge two boats, left there by the fishermen, who were washing their nets. He got into one of the boats, the one belonging to Simon, and asked him to put out a little from shore. Then he sat down and taught the people from the boat.

When he had finished speaking, he said to Simon, "Put out into deep water, and let down the nets for a catch."

Simon answered, "Master, we've worked hard all night and haven't caught anything. But because you say so, I will let down the nets."

When they had done so, they caught such a large number of fish that their nets began to break. So they signaled their partners in the other boat to come and help them, and they came and filled both boats so full that they began to sink.

When Simon Peter saw this, he fell at Jesus' knees and

said, "Go away from me, Lord; I am a sinful man!" For he
and all his companions were astonished at the catch of fish
they had taken, and so were James and John, the sons of
Zebedee, Simon's partners.

Then Jesus said to Simon, "Don't be afraid; from now
on you will fish for people." So they pulled their boats up
on shore, left everything and followed him.

—Luke 5:1–11

WE'VE ALL HEARD OF GOD WORKING MIRACLES for people in their jobs
and careers. Sure, sometimes these are the result of circumstantial events, but
often they are true-blue miracles—God stepping in and working something out.

A friend of mine (we'll call him Kevin) had enjoyed a long, successful career,
but the organization was making changes. A new guy was brought in with his
own ideas about how to do things. Kevin had done his job well for many years
but now was faced with a set of new circumstances, and this guy was telling him
what to do.

Kevin worked for a while with this new boss, but it didn't go well. Kevin felt
that the new guy's ideas were bypassing Kevin's expertise and were taking away
his control of projects.

I don't know all the circumstances, but eventually my friend was let go. He
felt like a failure even though he'd always been successful in his career and in this
particular job.

I know that many people have gone through this. Maybe you're going
through it now.

Kevin confided in me that, long before he was let go, he had come to feel
stuck in his job. Some of his responsibilities were tasks he had done for years,

and he admitted he was tired of doing them. His performance hadn't diminished, but his energy and enthusiasm for the job had waned. A lot of his work had become drudgery. He felt as if he had reached a plateau.

We've all been through this, haven't we? Whether in business or home or life in general, it's a common story. Everything goes well for a while. Then it flattens out. The success isn't there like it once was. More important, our enthusiasm isn't what it used to be. What once was an exciting mission is now just a lot of plain ol' work. Long hours and hard labor that aren't yielding satisfying results.

We've hit a plateau. We're empty. All our ideas and strategies have become old and tired and less successful.

Then the new guy comes in. The new guy could be a new boss or a new friend or your wife or husband or your mom or dad. He or she sees your frustration and, speaking usually with deep wisdom, has an idea.

"But," you say, "that's not how I do it."

And the new guy (boss or friend or spouse or parent) says, "Okay, but do it anyway."

And you have a choice to make.

COMING UP EMPTY

Simon Peter and his friends had been fishing all night long and had nothing to show for it. All night they had dragged their nets through the water. All night they had worked hard with absolutely no positive results. Production was down.

In Bible times, fishing was a team effort, not unlike what many of us experience in our places of work. It wasn't, by the way, the kind of fishing I do occasionally outside my office. In back of Woodlands Church is a small pond that some of the church members have stocked with fish—bass primarily. Sometimes people will go out there with a fishing rod and relax along the banks, casting and reeling.

But in Bible times, fishermen used nets. There were three types. The seine net had weights at one end and cork floats on the other. Fishermen would cast this net into the water and then, grabbing the floating part of the net, drag it toward shore. The circular-cast net was another type, usually about twenty-five feet in diameter. And the trammel net was a third type. This cleverly constructed series of nets allowed small fish to pass through while snaring larger fish.

In each case, fishermen in that day needed to wash their nets after using them. This meant cleaning the nets of debris, sticks, rubble, and grasses that clogged them. And this is what the fishermen were doing in this story when they encountered Jesus.

This event is recorded also in Matthew and Mark, but here in Luke the story is fleshed out. And it happened after the first events of Jesus's ministry. He had started teaching and preaching to crowds. He had cast out demons and healed the sick. Luke tells us "news about him spread through the whole countryside" (4:14).

Jesus's journeys took Him along the Sea of Galilee, and it was because of various events here that Jesus began to be known.

One day on His travels, He came upon these fishermen washing their nets. He would use boats along the shore as places to speak to the crowds, and this time He climbed into Simon Peter's boat to address the people. And Jesus asked him to put out a little from the shore.

Since Peter and the other fishermen were cleaning their nets, we might assume it was the end of their fishing day and they were tired. And certainly they were discouraged because they'd been out all night and hadn't caught a single fish.

It might be a little like pulling an all-nighter to write a school paper. By six in the morning, bleary-eyed and exhausted, you write the last word and finally stand up and walk away to get some more coffee. You come back sipping the hot brew and look at your computer screen, and it's blank. The computer has crashed. Did you save your paper? Oh, no! You try to reboot, and the computer doesn't turn on. Again you try, and—thank God! It starts up. You frantically log on and look for the paper you've just spent ten hours creating. And it's not there. A file by that name comes up, but there are no words.

That is how the fishermen felt. No fish after a hard night's work.

Empty nets and discouraged men.

The fishermen's nets were completely empty, but as we'll see, there was also a deeper emptiness. Their lives felt completely empty. But remember the Miracle Map. When you're at the end of your rope, you're in the perfect place for a miracle.

Simon Peter said, "Master, we've worked hard all night and haven't caught anything."

You can almost hear the frustration in his voice. The words "worked hard" come from the Greek word *kopiao,* which means "to be wearied." Simon Peter was saying, "We've got nothing left in the tank. We are worn out. We are burned out." We can almost imagine what Simon Peter was thinking: *We're professionals. This is the trade we know. We've spent our lives learning the art and science of fishing, and tonight we've hit rock bottom.* They were thoroughly discouraged.

They had fished all night, but however hard they tried, whatever strategies they employed, they came up with empty nets.

I believe this story says a lot about you and me as well. Just like my friend Kevin going through a career crisis, we sometimes reach a plateau. We're empty. Our ideas and strategies aren't working. Whether we are fishermen or senior analysts or just living our lives, we find ourselves hitting a long stretch where life remains about the same—frustrating, discouraging, and empty.

So often we try to control our circumstances, but we really can't. When we say, "I have a new strategy, and I can turn my life around," we're assuming we have the power to change our lives. But we really don't. When we try to fix a problem in our own strength, the result is usually frustration and even greater discouragement.

We've worked hard all night, and we have nothing to show for it.

But the difference between frustration and fulfillment is Jesus Christ.

The fishermen were about to learn this. Divine fulfillment had just stepped into their boat.

INVITE JESUS INTO YOUR EMPTINESS

These verses suggest that Jesus was, day by day, walking along the shores of the Sea of Galilee, speaking to crowds and performing amazing acts. That seems to be true. And some might think that on this particular morning Jesus just happened to walk along this part of the shore where some fishermen were struggling.

But we know better because we have the end of the miracle to tell us that this event on this morning utterly changed the lives of these fishermen. And we know from the rest of Scripture that Simon Peter would be the rock on which Jesus would build His church (see Matthew 16:18), and James and John would become part of the core of disciples who would help shape Jesus's ministry.

So this was no accident. Jesus did not just happen upon these men that morning. This was a divine appointment. He was looking for them. Not just any bunch of fishermen, but *these particular men.* All along, God was cooking up something for Simon Peter, James, and John—and you and me. Something that has nothing to do with fish but everything to do with fulfillment.

In other words, Jesus is looking for you. He wants a divine appointment with you. He has a destiny for you that is the most fulfilling job opportunity you could ever imagine.

This says a lot about the character of God. The Bible says Jesus came "to seek and to save the lost" (Luke 19:10, ESV). And we often use that verse to speak about how God seeks those who do not believe in Him. And while that's true, it's also true that He seeks you and me when we find ourselves lost in life. He's looking for those who are at a plateau in life, lost in no-longer-fulfilling jobs, wandering around in career-life frustration.

The Miracle Map tells us that God cares about us at these difficult points in life, that He has plans for us, that He wants to save us from the ongoing discouragement in our lives.

The passage also says that Jesus climbed into Simon Peter's boat.

Wouldn't you like to have been there, watching this unfold? I wonder what Simon Peter was thinking. A crowd of people trailed after Jesus, so Simon Peter must have wondered who the new guy was. Or maybe the news of Jesus's teaching and healing had gotten around and Simon Peter realized this was indeed that Jesus.

Jesus was looking for a place from which to speak. It was effective for Him to speak from a boat that put out from shore just a little ways because the water amplified the sound of His voice. Jesus had been doing this along the Sea of Galilee, and this was what He wanted to do now.

We might assume Jesus asked Simon Peter if He could step into his boat, saying that He needed to speak to the crowd and that the water would carry His voice better. And we might assume that Simon Peter said yes.

We don't know how that went down, and it's a little thing in the text, but I think it's a big deal.

You see, Simon Peter allowed Jesus to step into his boat.

And we know what the boat was to Simon Peter.

It was his life.

How about you? What does this miracle say about you? What does it reveal about you? What does it mean for you to invite Jesus into your boat? Your life? What might you invite Jesus into? Your mess? Your emptiness?

This miracle might never have happened if Simon Peter hadn't let Jesus use his boat. We don't know, of course, because God has ways we can't even dream of. And He sometimes works miracles in spite of us. But we know on this occasion Jesus was looking for Simon Peter, and Simon Peter let Him in. Then a miracle happened.

How many miracles do we never experience because we don't let Jesus into our boats? Do we find ourselves doubting that God can do something for us? Do we see our mess, our shortcomings, our failures, and get so discouraged that we don't even see Jesus approaching?

We know what this miracle says about the character of God. What does it say about your character and mine?

To answer that, we need to look at the first miracle Christ performed.

At a wedding in Cana, Jesus turned water into wine.[18] The host had run out of wine, and all the jars were empty. But Jesus filled the emptiness, because that's what Christ does: He fills our emptiness.

Think about this event for a moment. The smartest thing this couple ever did was to invite Jesus to their wedding. When they were writing out those invitations, maybe they were asking, "Should we invite, you know, Mary's son? What's his name—Jesus? I think he's about thirty now. I'm not sure what he's up to. I've heard he's an amazing teacher. I've heard some crazy things about him too. Maybe he's just insane. I don't know. But he can't be nearly as weird as, you know, Uncle Bill, so why don't we invite him?"

They invited Jesus. If you want a miracle, invite Christ into your life. Invite Christ into your marriage. Invite Christ into your business. Invite Christ into your family. Invite Christ into every area of your life.

And watch the miracles happen.

He is the Miracle Worker.

THE DEEP WATER OF SURRENDER

When he had finished speaking, he said to Simon, "Put out into deep water, and let down the nets for a catch." (Luke 5:4)

Note those words "deep water." Every professional fisherman knew that if you wanted to catch fish in the Sea of Galilee, you fished in the shallows in the cool of the night. But here Jesus said to Simon Peter, "I want you to go out into deep water in the heat of the day and fish."

It's like the new guy coming in and saying, "Let's do it this way."

"But," you say, "we've tried that before, and it doesn't work." And he replies, "Do it anyway."

I'm sure the fishermen that day were at least skeptical and maybe even angry that this Jesus had the gall to tell them how to fish.

But they did it anyway. Yes, Simon Peter offered a slight protest: "Master, we've worked hard all night and haven't caught anything." Then he quickly dropped his objection: "But because you say so, I will let down the nets."

And they did it.

And I ask why. What prompted these fishermen to follow this ridiculous advice from Jesus?

Two things come to mind.

For one thing, there was just something about Jesus. His manner, His speech, His bearing were different from anything they had encountered before. He conveyed authority, but it wasn't power He imposed on people. It was a quiet authority that came from somewhere else. And Jesus's words made people believe He was able to do remarkable things.

Maybe the fishermen had heard just enough through the chatter of the crowds to think this man was special. But quite likely they were disarmed by Him and compelled to obey.

For another thing, I think these fishermen were desperate. They'd fished all night and hadn't caught anything. They had nothing to lose by letting down their nets again, and they desperately needed that catch. They needed to pay the bills. They couldn't afford to spend the whole night fishing and not have anything to show for it. But it was also about life. A life that had plateaued. Fishing was hard work every day and night. There had to be something more. They were desperate for more. And all they had were empty nets.

For whatever reason, they obeyed. Remember principle five of the Miracle Map? Only God gives miracles, but you have to position yourself to receive them. These fishermen honored Jesus and obeyed.

Consider if they had said, "Not today, Jesus. We're too discouraged. We're just too worn out." They would have missed the miracle.

I wonder how many miracles I miss because I don't throw my net into the water of obedience? The fishermen probably weren't expecting much to happen, but Jesus in His grace blessed their imperfect faith and their obedience.

It was their empty nets that created so much discouragement, and that discouragement drove them to a place of desperation, and their desperation drove them to Jesus. The perfect place to receive a miracle is at the end of your rope, the place of desperation.

The emptiness we feel when we are on a plateau drives us to desperation, and our desperation drives us to Jesus Christ. Remember another key to the Miracle Map: miracles happen when we're at the end of our rope.

So if you're at a place of desperation right now, you are at the "X marks the spot" on God's Miracle Map. You're right where a miracle can happen because desperation comes before deliverance. You're right there to receive God's miracle because your desperation has driven you to the source of fulfillment.

Shortly after this, Jesus delivered His most famous speech: the Sermon on the Mount. Luke reported that the crowds had assembled from surrounding regions. Then we read: "He went down with them and stood on a level place" (6:17).

Jesus came down from the mountainside and stood with them on the plateau, on the level place, where they were.

And Jesus is with us when we find ourselves on a plateau. When we are exhausted and tired and frustrated, when our lives are endless routine, when our nets are empty, Jesus stands with us in our discouragement and despair.

And there He says, "You're blessed when you're at the end of your rope. With less of you there is more of God and his rule" (Matthew 5:3, MSG). And He says, "Blessed are those who hunger and thirst for righteousness, for they will be filled" (Matthew 5:6).

So invite God into your emptiness. Be willing, as Peter was, to admit that you've been fishing all night and your nets are empty. Even as a follower of Jesus, you need to embrace and confess to Him your emptiness. When you come to the place of surrender, you'll discover the deep water of divine fulfillment.

EMPTY YOUR PRIDE

Recently I was invited by producer Mark Burnett to be his guest at a taping of the hit NBC television show *The Voice.* You know Mark Burnett and his wife, Roma Downey, from their many successful reality TV shows, including *Survivor, Shark Tank,* and *The Apprentice.* You may have seen their Bible miniseries *A.D. The Bible Continues.* It's been a privilege for us to become acquainted with Mark and Roma.

The Voice has been a favorite show in our household, so it was a special thrill to attend one of the shows and watch it live. After the show was over, my son Ryan and I had the opportunity to walk on the set. We took some pictures, and there's one of me sitting in Adam Levine's chair. I think I was hoping that some of Levine's talent would rub off on me—or at least a measure of his good looks. Or even just his hair! But, no, that was one miracle that didn't happen. Nor did I magically become a member of Maroon 5.

I think, though, I learned a life lesson as I sat in one of those big red captain's chairs on the set. I could sit in that captain's chair, but it didn't make me a great musician. I could pretend I had the power to control the destinies of wannabe singers, but that didn't give me musical talent either. Likewise, I can try to sit in the captain's chair of my life, but that doesn't make me God.

Yet that's exactly what we so often try to do.

Like my friend Kevin, who was on a career plateau, we so often attempt to control our lives by preserving the status quo or trying some new strategy to save ourselves or saying that we can't change because "we've always done it this way."

That is our pride talking, and it prevents us from experiencing God's miracles and discovering His purposes for us.

There's a little more to Simon Peter's response to Jesus that we need to know. Peter's words were "Master, we've worked hard all night and haven't caught anything." The word for "Master" in Greek actually means "respected teacher," and the emphasis here suggests that Simon Peter was actually using the term as a backhanded compliment, maybe with a touch of sarcasm. Perhaps he was saying, "Jesus, you are a master teacher. You're a great teacher. You're great at the spiritual stuff. You know a lot about teaching, but you don't know anything about fishing. It's fine for you to stand in my boat and teach people, but I'm the professional fisherman. Leave it to the professionals. That's my business, and stay out of my business." We know Peter's personality from other parts of Scripture. He was often impetuous, brash, and self-promoting. So it is not much of a stretch to imagine that his words to Jesus had this tone and implication.

We also have to deal with our pride and a desire to establish and emphasize our own greatness and a desire to control our lives. We are Kevin and Simon Peter rolled into one.

At least Simon Peter, despite his pride, obeyed Jesus. Peter said, "Because you say so, I will let down the nets." But I believe Peter obeyed only on the outside and on the inside was still full of pride. I interpret his words to mean, "Okay, Jesus, I'll do this, but it's a real waste of time. I'm going to do this because I don't want to offend You, but this is ridiculous. It's not going to work, and I'll show You."

Peter dropped the nets into the deep water, and *boom!* The miracle happened. He got a boatload of fish. Well, really two boatloads of fish. The nets started to tear. The boats started to sink.

That's God's sense of humor. He knew what Simon Peter was thinking, and it's as if God's response was "Yeah, you don't think this is going to happen, do you? Well, you know I was just going to give you a nice catch of fish. Now I'm going to give you so much it will start to sink the boat."

And that's what happened in this amazing miracle. I love that obedience brought blessing to Peter even though in his heart he was likely pretty cynical.

Jesus filled Simon Peter's nets, but He couldn't fill Simon Peter's life until the fisherman emptied himself of his pride. And that's what happened after the miracle. Before the miracle Peter was full of pride, but God still worked the miracle. And after the miracle Peter was a humbled man, emptied of ego. Look at what verse 8 says: "When Simon Peter saw this, he fell at Jesus' knees and said, 'Go away from me, Lord; I am a sinful man!'"

The Greek word for "Lord" here is *kurios,* and it means "controller of everything." Notice that a few minutes earlier Peter had been saying, "You are a master teacher. You're in control when you're teaching about spiritual things." Here he's saying, "You are the controller of everything. You are a master fisherman. I am not worthy. Forgive me."

And in the moment Jesus took over Peter's business, He took over Peter's life as well. And Simon Peter's ego was emptied out.

You see, God can't fill you with His provision and purpose until your ego is poured out of your life.

I think it's interesting that we can be desperate and prideful at the same time. That might have been true of my friend Kevin. He was desperate, trapped on a plateau in the middle of drudgery, yet he was resistant to new ways of doing things, to changes in a process that wasn't broken, and to help from another person who had a different idea. Peter had labored with the others all night doing what he was trained to do, performing his professional expertise in fishing, yet staring into empty nets in the morning, and he was faced with utter failure. He was desperate, but he pridefully responded to this Jesus-with-a-better-idea.

As you look to find your miracle, invite Jesus into your mess and emptiness. Let go of your pride and your desire to control the outcome. (It's not as if your control of everything has gone so well.) Remember the Miracle Map's third principle: *God works the miracle in His way and in His time.* You see, if you are full of pride, you can't be full of Jesus. When you come to the place where you surrender to God's infinite wisdom and love, He floods you with a supernatural peace that washes away the despair.

SURRENDER YOURSELF TO A NEW PURPOSE

Chip and Belinda Burkitt experienced a miracle in their lives that is still unfolding. Parents of six, they had sometimes struggled to make ends meet. Chip, though, was able to land a good job in a software company. For once they had a steady income.

However, after three years Chip received the news: he was being laid off. But in the aftermath of this devastating news, Chip and his family found an envelope full of money slipped under their door. A close friend left a gift card in their freezer. Friends supplied groceries, gas cards, shoes, and so much more over months of great need.

Belinda says that, despite everything, they've managed to pay down their credit cards and stay reasonably current on their mortgage. "We consider this a miracle," she adds.

The experience has not only brought Chip and Belinda closer together, but it's brought them closer to God and to other people. Belinda writes, "Chip and I have prayed together and read the Bible almost every morning for about two years. . . . Not just out of discipline, but out of necessity."[19]

I think God surprises us with abundant blessing when we let go of empty nets.

Luke 5:11 says, "So they pulled their boats up on shore, left everything and followed him." Notice the two words "left everything." They surrendered their profession. They surrendered their possessions. They surrendered their plans.

When we hold on to our little perfect plan that we try to orchestrate and control and micromanage, we get frustrated if things don't seem to work out. We find ourselves on a plateau of discouragement, and we try even harder to control our lives, yet all the while we just pull in empty nets. The more we try to control something, the more it spins out of control, the more frustrated we get, and we are left empty. But when we surrender to God's plan, everything begins to change. He begins to fill us up with peace and purpose. He begins to meet our needs.

When God takes control of our lives, we receive two things: a bigger vision and a higher purpose. Jesus started with the miracle they thought they needed most—full nets—and it led them to what they really needed most. A relationship with Christ.

First, God gives us *a bigger vision*.

Luke 5:6–7 says, "They caught such a large number of fish that their nets began to break. So they signaled their partners in the other boat to come and help them, and they came and filled both boats so full that they began to sink."

Later the passage says the fishermen "were astonished at the catch." I love that word *astonished*. God loves to astonish us with His miracles. I imagine He thought, *I'm going to amaze these guys! I'm going to do something astonishing! I'm going to blow them out of the water! Literally!*

God loves to open our eyes to what He can do in our lives. I think Belinda and Chip Burkitt found that out. When Chip lost his job, life got very hard for them, and it pushed them into another dimension of spiritual connection with God, a deeper faith, and a more fervent prayer life. And they soon were astonished to see how God provided.

The first thing God does when He fills up your life is open your eyes. He expands your vision to see what He can do in your life. He changes your focus from what you can't do to what He can do. And you can say with Paul, "I can do all things through Christ who strengthens me" (Philippians 4:13, NKJV).

Maybe you've been content to catch minnows because that's all you've known. Perhaps you've been content to play in a mud puddle because you can't even imagine what the ocean of God's provision and miracles and purpose looks like. God wants to open your eyes, first to see how empty your nets really are and then to see how full His astonishing provision can make them.

When you let go, open up, and surrender to God, He opens your eyes to see a whole new world. He gives you a bigger vision. He wants your nets to be so full they almost sink your boat.

God also gives you *a higher purpose*. Verse 11 says, "Then Jesus said to Simon, 'Don't be afraid; from now on you will fish for people.'"

Simon Peter and the others were still fishermen, but from here on they were going to fish for changed lives. Whether you're an accountant, or an athlete, or a businesswoman, or a stay-at-home mom or dad, or a CEO, or a pizza delivery guy, when you let go of your life and open yourself to the miracle God has for you, God is there saying, "Don't be afraid. I have a higher purpose for you. I want you to be the gospel to the people in your life. I want you to reflect the light of Christ around you."

God has this high calling for your life, and until you let Him fill your life nets to the point of breaking with astonishing abundance, you'll never really see that higher purpose. You'll never really see that what you're doing will last for all eternity.

After more than a year of searching, Chip found a job. As Belinda says, "From the best to the worst, and every ordinary day in between, God has been there." And if you doubt that God was really working a miracle in the lives of the Burkitt family, consider this: Chip got his new job the same week his unemployment benefits ran out.[20]

Sometimes we choose to let go of our empty nets in order to follow God's bigger vision and higher purpose, as the disciples did. Sometimes, as with my friend Kevin, God plunges us into uncertainty so we will seek the only certainty in life: God Himself. And sometimes God takes control of our lives unexpectedly, as He did with the Burkitts, and opens up opportunities for us to see a bigger vision of life and a higher purpose.

As you seek the miracle you need right now, know that your empty nets, your plateaued life, and those waves of discouragement are great opportunities for Jesus to walk by and turn your life gloriously and astonishingly upside down.

Promises for When You're Discouraged

Let us not become weary in doing good, for at the proper time we will reap a harvest if we do not give up.

Galatians 6:9

For we live by faith, not by sight.

2 Corinthians 5:7

If you only look at us, you might well miss the brightness. We carry this precious Message around in the unadorned clay pots of our ordinary lives. That's to prevent anyone from confusing God's incomparable power with us. As it is, there's not much chance of that. You know for yourselves that we're not much to look at. We've been surrounded and battered by troubles, but we're not demoralized; we're not sure what to do, but we know that God knows what to do; we've been spiritually terrorized, but God hasn't left our side; we've been thrown down, but we haven't broken. What they did to Jesus, they do to us—trial and torture, mockery and murder; what Jesus did among them, he does in us—he lives! Our lives are at constant risk for Jesus' sake, which makes Jesus' life all the more evident in us. While we're going through the worst, you're getting in on the best!

2 Corinthians 4:8–12, MSG

If God is for us, who can be against us?

Romans 8:31

For the Lord will not forsake his people, for his great name's sake, because it has pleased the Lord to make you a people for himself.

1 Samuel 12:22, ESV

Do not let your hearts be troubled. You believe in God; believe also in me.

John 14:1

Who shall separate us from the love of Christ? Shall trouble or hardship or persecution or famine or nakedness or danger or sword? As it is written:

"For your sake we face death all day long;
    we are considered as sheep to be slaughtered."

No, in all these things we are more than conquerors through him who loved us.

Romans 8:35–37

I have told you these things, so that in me you may have peace. In this world you will have trouble. But take heart! I have overcome the world.

John 16:33

Jesus: The Storm Chaser

We cannot rely on ourselves, for we have learned from bitter experience the folly of self-confidence. We are compelled to look to the Lord alone. Blessed is the wind that drives the ship into the harbor. Blessed is the distress that forces us to rest in our God.

—Charles Spurgeon

Hardship often prepares an ordinary person for an extra-ordinary destiny.

—C. S. Lewis

8

When You're Afraid

Jesus Calms the Storm

That day when evening came, he said to his disciples, "Let us go over to the other side." Leaving the crowd behind, they took him along, just as he was, in the boat. There were also other boats with him. A furious squall came up, and the waves broke over the boat, so that it was nearly swamped. Jesus was in the stern, sleeping on a cushion. The disciples woke him and said to him, "Teacher, don't you care if we drown?"

He got up, rebuked the wind and said to the waves, "Quiet! Be still!" Then the wind died down and it was completely calm.

He said to his disciples, "Why are you so afraid? Do you still have no faith?"

They were terrified and asked each other, "Who is this? Even the wind and the waves obey him!"

—Mark 4:35–41

IN 1958 A HUGE CARGO SHIP was built, a freighter that at the time was the largest ever to sail the Great Lakes. It was two football fields long, some seventy-five feet wide, and more than three stories tall. The enormity of the ship, its steel construction, and its swift speed made it the envy of the shipping industry in its day. Designed to haul iron ore from Minnesota to the automobile factories in Detroit, the ship was expected to last more than fifty years.

Nicknamed "The Queen of the Great Lakes," the freighter was the first to be commissioned and built by an insurance company. Even though it hauled iron ore, its living spaces were decorated luxuriously with pile carpet, drapes over the portholes, tiled bathrooms, and leather chairs. On its frequent voyages, the ship could entertain the insurance company VIPs and their friends with champagne dinners in posh rooms.

The ship became a favorite of people along the shores of the Great Lakes. When it passed close to shore, Captain Peter Pulcer, a bit of a showman, would blast music over the intercom. Sometimes he would get on his bullhorn and, playing tour guide, broadcast facts and trivia about the great ship to the people on shore.

For nearly two decades "The Queen of the Great Lakes" hauled tons of marble-shaped iron ore across Lake Superior and Lake Huron. It broke records for speed, number of trips, and quantities of cargo. While the rest of the world didn't much know about it, the ship became the pride of the region.

In November 1975, not quite two decades after its launch, the great ship was on yet another trip from Minnesota to Detroit. The weather forecast was normal for November—cold and choppy but nothing unusual. A small storm brewing off Lake Superior was passing south and would be of no consequence.

What would make this particular voyage special was that it would mark the retirement of Captain Ernest McSorley. He had just turned sixty-three and was planning to leave behind his long, successful career.

That night the ship, also known as "The Fitz" after the insurance company president who commissioned it, ran into trouble. A storm hit suddenly. It was quick and violent, unleashing hurricane-force winds and thirty-five-foot waves.

What might have been just a regional tragedy became more broadly known a year later through the lyrics of a song composed by Canadian folk singer Gordon Lightfoot—"The Wreck of the Edmund Fitzgerald." Haunting and sad, the song tells the tale of this ship that was "the pride of the American side," the invincible freighter that should have lasted fifty years but was tragically done in by a sudden storm on Lake Superior.

The *Edmund Fitzgerald* sank. There were no survivors.

The last words heard from Captain McSorley were broadcast to a sister ship not far away: "We are holding our own."

The Storms of Our Lives

How often do we sail through stretches of life and think we're doing just fine? How often do we float through circumstances and feel we're in charge, captain of our own invincible ship? How often do we say confidently to others, "Yep, I know what I'm doing. I've got it covered. I'm holding my own"?

Is that security for real? Or, as we journey through life, do we let our security default to the steel hull of a steady job, good health, and a comfortable lifestyle? And is our safe, posh, secure existence really just an illusion?

A storm hits. Suddenly our world is thrown into disarray. Suddenly the boat we're in isn't stable anymore. Suddenly the deck is tilting, waves are crashing against our ship, and we're flooded with uncontrollable fear.

Suddenly all our security is gone. What do we do?

Is this the situation you find yourself in right now? Maybe you lost a job. Perhaps your marriage is crashing and burning. Or maybe you've lost someone close to you. Or a health issue has surfaced. A secret habit or addiction has been discovered. Yes, these are the storms of life that jolt us out of our false security.

We tremble in the face of them and panic as we realize how weak and vulnerable we really are.

There's one line of the Lightfoot song that haunts me: "Does any one know where the love of God goes when the waves turn the minutes to hours?"

The valleys of life lead us to cry out, "Why have You forgotten me, God?"

The plateaus of life lead us to cry out, "How much longer, God?"

The mountains of life lead us to cry out, "How can I make it, God?"

But it's the storms of life that lead us to cry out, "Where are You, God? Where has Your love gone?"

Two thousand years before the tragedy of the *Edmund Fitzgerald,* a group of men boarded a much smaller boat to cross the Sea of Galilee. And it was at this time and place that a miracle happened, one that speaks into the storm of fear you face today.

Sailing into a Miracle

Jesus told His disciples that He wanted to take the boat "to the other side." He had just finished the series of teachings that we know as the Sermon on the Mount. It was an intense time of brilliant teaching for His disciples, speaking to crowds, and admonishing the Pharisees. The Sermon on the Mount was a thought-and-word explosion that today informs the core of Christian theology.

If we follow the legend of the Miracle Map, specifically the principle of what a miracle reveals about Jesus and God, here we see that Jesus needed some downtime, which makes a strong statement about His humanity. Of course He was God as well, but here we see the human side. He was tired and needed rest. Just a few verses later, we learn that Jesus fell asleep on the boat.

As they were halfway across the lake, a huge storm came up suddenly and surprised the disciples. It caught them totally unaware.

At some point as I was reading this passage, I had an aha! moment. Something became clear to me. In my research I read that at this time the Jews as a people were generally landlubbers. They made their living off the land, and even though some were fishermen, as a people they weren't known for seafaring. In fact, some scholars say the Jews were given to water-related fears and thought the sea was filled with all kinds of dangerous creatures.

But we know that some of the disciples were fishermen. We expect that they had experience with weather on the Sea of Galilee, that they might have spotted storms of this kind. In fact, we might expect they could spot a storm from far off and, if so, would avoid fishing that day.

Yet we hear nothing in the passage about the experienced fishermen among the disciples recognizing that a storm was brewing. They didn't know or suspect a thing.

But Jesus did.

Being God, Jesus knew that they would encounter a storm crossing the Sea of Galilee. In fact, He was *counting* on it. Indeed, that was His plan all along.

The legend on the Miracle Map tells us that God does the miracle His way, and it's usually a way that no one is expecting. Who would expect God to chart a course *into* a storm!

See, many times when we're in the storms of life, we think that God is mad at us or that He's trying to get back at us. Maybe we think He has stopped loving us.

But most of the time the problem isn't that we're going the wrong direction. It's that God has directed us right into the middle of the storm, which is right where He wants us. Along our life journey, storms may seem unpredictable, but in God's plan they are *purposeful*.

God doesn't cause evil to happen to us, but evil exists. It's part of our fallen world. We want God to protect us from bad things in life, yet sometimes He allows us to experience them. At times He allows the pain, He allows the trouble, He allows the problem to rise up. He allows the storm and sometimes even leads us into it.

But, you see, God never wastes a storm. He never wastes a teardrop. There is a purpose behind every problem in your life, and many times that very problem is an opportunity for God to work a miracle. Many times the storm is the very barrier that becomes the blessing that directs us to our calling.

One of the reasons God leads us into a storm is to intentionally move us out of our *comfort* zone and into His *miracle* zone. Jesus said, "Get into the boat. Let's go to the other side." He knew a storm was out there, waiting for them, but He didn't give them a choice. "We're going," He said. He didn't say, "Well, there's a storm out there, so you can go with Me or stay here in the comfort of the shore." He didn't give them a choice because they might have chosen to stay.

Sometimes God doesn't give us a choice either. Instead He directs us right into a storm. It comes unexpectedly into our lives, but He knew about it all along, and it's part of His plan, because it's only in the storms that we grow. It's only in the challenges, only in the problems that we turn to Him and experience the miracle. It's in the moments when we are flooded with fear that we find our faith strengthened.

No one chooses problems. I would never choose any of the problems that have come into my life. I would never choose any of the hurts that have come into my life. I would never choose to go through the storms in my life. You and I want to be comfortable, and many times we make it our number-one goal in life to be comfortable, to be safe, to be secure, to eliminate all risk. Yet all we've done is kill ourselves a little at a time. We let all the passion drain out of our lives.

If your goal is to be comfortable, safe, and secure, you're not living by faith, and "without faith it is impossible to please God" (Hebrews 11:6). Faith and challenge and risk make us come alive and open us to experiencing a miracle. The miracle happens in the middle of the storm, and God knows He has to use storms to shove us out of our comfort zone, the death zone, into the miracle zone, where we can experience the miracle that we otherwise would miss. Storms don't come because God is mad at you. They come because He loves you and wants you to experience a miracle.

God doesn't give us a choice. He knows we would always choose the comfort of pile carpet and leather chairs in the VIP lounge. So God allows us to sail into the storms.

The Fear of God

Crossing the Sea of Galilee was often treacherous in Bible times.

Some translations call this body of water a lake. But as a lake, it's of some size—roughly thirty-one miles long and eight miles wide. In fact, it's the largest freshwater lake in Israel and the lowest freshwater lake on earth at 680 feet below sea level.

The Sea of Galilee was famous for its sudden, rough storms. The climate is affected by the nearby mountains—Mount Hermon to the north and Mount Arbel to the west. The temperature and pressure differences between the cool, dry mountain air and the warm, moist air of the lake result in strong winds that descend on the Sea of Galilee and kick up violent storms.

So one such violent storm arose. The Greek word in Scripture for this storm is *seismos,* from which we get our word *seismic,* and it means "shaking." This storm churned up the waters and shook the boat and its passengers. I imagine the disciples were unable to see even a few feet in front of them as the rain blew sideways and the waves broke over the boat—maybe ten or fifteen feet high.

In the midst of their fear, the loud crashing of the storm, and the water cascading over them, they go to the stern of the boat, desperate for Jesus. And they find Him sleeping. He is snoozing in the midst of chaos. I like the detail the Bible gives us—that Jesus was "sleeping on a cushion."

I think the disciples acted just as we do when we're facing the violent storms of life, knee-deep in rising seawater fear. We wonder if God is sleeping on the job. And we wonder if He has allowed these things to happen.

The disciples woke up Jesus. "Teacher, don't you care if we drown?" They were in despair, their belief in Jesus greatly shaken by the storm. *"Does any one know where the love of God goes when the waves turn the minutes to hours?"*

I see myself in this scene. How often do I allow the events of life to shake my faith in Jesus's love for me? How about you? Does that sound familiar? Do you find yourself in the midst of a storm reaching out desperately to shake a sleeping Jesus?

So Jesus awoke. We don't know how long it took the disciples to rouse Him. We don't know anything else He said. I imagine He opened His eyes, fully aware of what was happening. Maybe He was disappointed at the disciples' response to the situation. If I were writing the Hollywood script, I'd have Jesus say, "Hey, guys. Really? You think God is going to let this boat sink while His Son is in it?"

Of course we don't have the transcript of that conversation. (It certainly wouldn't be any cheesy Hollywood dialogue!) Instead, we're told "He got up, rebuked the wind and said to the waves, 'Quiet! Be still!'"

The storm stopped. Within seconds the Sea of Galilee was like glass. *Suddenly.*

Now here we go to the Miracle Map to apply one of its principles. As we know, miracles are not always about what they're about. And we're also aware that physical miracles activate heart miracles. So we might logically think that this miracle is about Jesus taking control of the storm, of the sea, of nature. And, yes, it has that meaning, and that is very important. It goes to the very essence of what miracles are—how God, who is outside of nature, sometimes enters into nature to change something.

This is obviously and literally true here. Jesus literally stopped the storm in its tracks. That is certainly what the disciples reacted to when they said, "Who is this? Even the wind and the waves obey him!"

But what else is this miracle about?

Certainly it's about the disciples themselves. The Bible says that even after Jesus calmed the storm, "they were terrified." Did the miracle remove their fear? No, it simply redirected their fear. Now, instead of fearing a storm, they were afraid of *Jesus*. "Who is this?" they asked among themselves. And maybe this redirected fear was a fear of what following Jesus really meant. Between their horrified gazes into the teeth of the storm and their puzzled looks into the eyes of Jesus, they caught a glimpse of the power and holiness of God.

They no longer were afraid of the storm, because they began to experience the fear of God, which is a very helpful and healthy fear. In fact, Solomon told us in Proverbs, the book of wisdom, "The fear of the LORD is the beginning of wisdom" (9:10). Scripture is telling us that the first step to making wise decisions is to fear God.

Yet the term *fear of the Lord* is misunderstood by most people today. That's because many people, when they think about God, get scared. They fear His judgment of their sin, and they think God is a cosmic kill-joy who wants to steal all their fun and takes great joy in punishing their missteps.

Some people are scared of God because they are scared of pastors! When we started our church, I helped coach my son's soccer team. At the first couple of practices, I was getting to know the other dads and having a great time with them. After a couple of weeks, one of the other dads asked me what I did for a living. I said, "Well, I'm the pastor of a new church in the area." His eyes got huge! You could just sense his thoughts shuffling back through everything he'd said to me in the last two weeks. I'm sure he was thinking, *Oh no! Did I cuss? I didn't know he was a pastor. I thought he was normal, but he's a pastor!* If people are afraid to be around pastors, I know many are definitely afraid of God.

The fear of God, however, doesn't mean that you should be scared of Him and run from Him. No. It means you're so in awe of God that you run *to* Him and bow *before* Him. If you're a Christ follower, you don't have to be scared of God, because Christ took your judgment on the cross. He was condemned so you wouldn't be.

The fear of God is not a fear of judgment. It's a reverence and awe of God.

It's recognizing His greatness, holiness, power, and love and responding to Him with humility and honor.

One of the most overused words in modern English is *awesome*. We use it to describe a meal or a sporting event or a movie. But really there is only One who deserves and demands our awe, and He deserves more than some awe. He deserves all our awe. When we consider how great and powerful God is, we are filled with awe, and our fears start to fade.

When I fear God, my fear of what people think starts to evaporate. When I fear God, my fears about the storms of life begin to dissipate. If you fear God, all your other fears start to recede.

When the disciples began to fear God, all their other fears were gone.

I love that Jesus asked them, "Why are you so afraid? Do you still have no faith?" I can feel the love in that question as Jesus was saying, essentially, "Hey, guys, I want you to believe and trust in Me so you won't be paralyzed by fear."

God wants to replace our fears in life with awe of Him.

When a storm slams into our lives, we react in fear. We cry out, wondering where God is. We suspect He's sleeping, not paying attention, or, worse, that He no longer loves us. We become desperate for Jesus yet act as if He's really not there for us.

And then the storm stops. Not always, I know, but often God intervenes in the storms of our lives and rescues us. Suddenly He is there. Suddenly the wind and waves cease. *Suddenly.* He opens a way out of our circumstances or pain or predicament. Jesus says, "Be still!" and the storm goes away.

But then don't we look into Jesus's eyes and see something else? Don't we see what He wants from us? Don't we see His disappointment at our lack of faith, our shallow commitment to Him, our superficial and comfortable leather-chair-on-pile-carpet level of discipleship?

Jesus says to you and me, "I can take care of the storms in your life. But I'm in the process of changing the world here. I need you to step up. Yes, following Me is hard. It's costly. Are you in?"

IS JESUS IN YOUR BOAT?

University of Texas football coach Darrell Royal led the Longhorns through two successful and competitive decades. He's also known for colloquial sayings that captured people's fancy. One was "You've got to think lucky. If you fall into a mudhole, check your back pocket. You might have caught a fish."

He was also known for saying "You gotta dance with the one who brung ya." While he didn't originate that, he popularized it in sports. It means that in the big game you have to trust the talent that has won for you during the season.

The saying also applies to this miracle.

The Mark 4 passage says, "Leaving the crowd behind, they took him along, just as he was, in the boat." It's a simple and obvious thing but so important. Apparently Jesus had been preaching to the crowd along the shore. He'd used the boat itself as a kind of platform. When He and His disciples prepared to cross the Sea of Galilee, they "took him along, just as he was, in the boat."

The simple truth here is that *Jesus was with them.*

I think we can glean several practical insights from this.

First, we must be clear about *who Jesus is.* At this point the disciples were not. It's understandable that the disciples were terrified of this intense storm. We would be too. It's understandable that they'd become impatient with Jesus sleeping in the stern of the boat while the boat was being battered by wind and waves. But when they addressed Him out of their fear, they called Him "Teacher," and their demeanor, fear, and trembling suggested they didn't quite know or believe who He was—that He was God Himself. And when He indeed stopped the storm in its tracks, they couldn't believe it. Because they really didn't understand or believe who Jesus was.

We might give the disciples a break. They hadn't known Jesus for very long at the time of this miracle. We have the benefit of the whole Bible and years of Christian teaching to guide us into a knowledge of who Jesus is. During the period of time covered by the Gospels, the disciples seemed to gradually grasp the true identity of Jesus, but maybe at this early point in His ministry, they were still trying to put things together.

We don't have that same excuse. Jesus is with us in the boat, but do we really know and believe and trust that Jesus is indeed God? Do we really believe that He can work miracles in our lives and stop the storms by His command? Do we really believe in the power of Jesus, who is God, in our lives?

Second, we need to embrace the truth that *there is no storm I'll face alone.*

Mark 4:36 is interesting: "They took him along." Of course Jesus knew perfectly well that there would be a terrible storm. And He knew exactly how this experience, this miracle, would further shape the hearts of His disciples. So perhaps in a literal sense the disciples took Jesus along, but we know what the disciples didn't know—that Jesus engineered all of this. He brought them along.

When we face the storms of life, we need to be careful we don't get this confused. Sure, we may find ourselves in a storm and then, almost as an afterthought, remember to bring Jesus into it, to bring Him along. But that means we're using Jesus, in a way, as a cosmic Problem Solver. That's not the way He works. Instead, we must understand He's the One who knows what is coming and He's the One who brought us along, not the other way around. He wants us simply to trust in Him.

We need to rest in the Jesus who brung us.

Truth is, believers and nonbelievers go through a lot of the same things in life. Now some people will tell you that if you commit your life to Christ, everything will be perfect. You'll have no more problems. Everything will be great. Smooth sailing. Yeah, right. But that's just not the case, because we live in a broken world. We're not in heaven yet, the perfect place. One day everything will perfect, but right now there are problems and sin and hurt and pain and stresses and tragedy. Believers and nonbelievers experience all the same things. We all face storms.

But there's one big difference.

If you're a Christ follower, you have the assurance that He's in the boat with you. You can trust that you will never go through anything alone. You and I will never face any problem on our own.

And, ultimately, knowing who Jesus really is and being assured there's no storm we will go through alone, we can also know that being in the boat with Jesus means *there's no storm that will take us under.*

God is not going to sink the boat with Jesus in it. And Jesus is in your boat. It may feel as if you're going under. You may take on some water. You may get wet. Your boat may get battered and beaten by the storm, but you will not drown. You will not go under. Jesus will see you through.

I love this passage from Isaiah 43:

Do not be afraid, for I have ransomed you.
　I have called you by name; you are mine.
When you go through deep waters,
　I will be with you.
When you go through rivers of difficulty,
　you will not drown. . . .
　You are honored, and I love you.

Do not be afraid, for I am with you. (verses 1–2, 4–5, NLT)

Maybe for you the miracle of Jesus's calming the storm raises the question of who Jesus is. And maybe that question is echoing right now in the storm you're facing. Whether the storm is in your career, your family, your friendships, or your personal struggles, the simple question is this: Is Jesus Christ in the boat with you? Are you a Christ follower? Have you prayed to receive Christ?

Maybe for you the miracle of Jesus's calming the storm is a matter of discipleship. Maybe you've been more like the disciples were, trading their fear of the storm for fear of God. Perhaps the miracle calls you to look into Jesus's eyes, accept the cost of following Him, and allow Him to radically take your life to the next level.

Or maybe for you the miracle of Jesus's calming the storm is a matter of simply surviving the storm you find yourself in. You may feel as if you're going under for the last time. But God says, "No, I'm in the boat with you, and you will not drown. You might get wet, but you will not drown. You might need to go through the storm, but you will not drown."

As you look to find your miracle today, understand that the miracle God has for you might not mean escaping the storm you're in but going through it with Him. The miracle might be that, by going through the storm, your experience of Jesus will be deeper and richer than you ever thought possible.

Promises for When You're Afraid

For God has not given us a spirit of fear and timidity, but of power, love, and self-discipline.

2 Timothy 1:7, NLT

What time I am afraid, I will trust in thee.

Psalm 56:3, KJV

Do not be afraid, for I have ransomed you.
  I have called you by name; you are mine.
When you go through deep waters,
  I will be with you.
When you go through rivers of difficulty,
  you will not drown.
When you walk through the fire of oppression,
  you will not be burned up;
  the flames will not consume you.

Isaiah 43:1–2, NLT

Do not be afraid, little flock, for your Father has been pleased to give you the kingdom.

Luke 12:32

The angel of the LORD encamps around those who fear him,
  and he delivers them.

Psalm 34:7

I am leaving you with a gift—peace of mind and heart. And the peace I give is a gift the world cannot give. So don't be troubled or afraid.

John 14:27, NLT

I prayed to the LORD, and he answered me.
> He freed me from all my fears.

Psalm 34:4, NLT

Perfect love expels all fear. If we are afraid, it is for fear of punishment, and this shows that we have not fully experienced his perfect love.

1 John 4:18, NLT

But Jesus overheard them and said to Jairus, "Don't be afraid. Just have faith."

Mark 5:36, NLT

I, yes I, am the one who comforts you.
> So why are you afraid of mere humans,
> who wither like the grass and disappear?

Isaiah 51:12, NLT

9

When You're Lonely

Jesus Walks on Water

Meanwhile, the disciples were in trouble far away from land, for a strong wind had risen, and they were fighting heavy waves. About three o'clock in the morning Jesus came toward them, walking on the water. When the disciples saw him walking on the water, they were terrified. In their fear, they cried out, "It's a ghost!"

But Jesus spoke to them at once. "Don't be afraid," he said. "Take courage. I am here!"

Then Peter called to him, "Lord, if it's really you, tell me to come to you, walking on the water."

"Yes, come," Jesus said.

So Peter went over the side of the boat and walked on the water toward Jesus. But when he saw the strong wind and the waves, he was terrified and began to sink. "Save me, Lord!" he shouted.

Jesus immediately reached out and grabbed him. "You have so little faith," Jesus said. "Why did you doubt me?"

> When they climbed back into the boat, the wind
> stopped. Then the disciples worshiped him. "You really are
> the Son of God!" they exclaimed.
>
> —Matthew 14:24–33, NLT

THIS IS A MIRACLE about feeling alone in the face of fear. It's a miracle about Jesus being present with you and me in the storms of life. And it's a miracle about the power of faith to bring to you the miracle you need right now.

In 2000 a movie told the true story of New England fishermen who were at the tail end of the fishing season. They'd had disappointing results in their previous expeditions. The captain of the ship, played by George Clooney, convinces the crew to go out with him one last time in hopes of getting a successful catch. They all board the fishing boat, the *Andrea Gail,* and set out onto the Atlantic. They do, in fact, run into a good catch, and the expedition appears successful—until they head back home. As it happens, their return trip takes them directly into the path of a nor'easter. That would have been bad enough, but this nor'easter had just intersected with a hurricane, ironically known as Hurricane Grace. This real-life storm of 1991 became known as "the perfect storm," also the title of the movie. I guess we're past the point of a spoiler alert, so I'll just say it doesn't end well.

In the stories of the *Andrea Gail* and the *Edmund Fitzgerald,* I find myself thinking about how lonely life at sea must be. I suppose on placid waters under a sunny sky, it might be quiet and relaxing, but even then it seems to me that the vastness of lakes, seas, and oceans would leave me feeling very alone. And how much more alone—and desperate—would I feel in the midst of a storm? With winds swirling, waves crashing, and the sound deafening, I would feel desperately alone. I think about that and realize that I feel that way when I'm in the storms of life. How quickly in the midst of those crashing waves I get to feeling so desperately alone.

Unlike the story of the *Andrea Gail,* this biblical account in Matthew didn't take place on the Atlantic Ocean but on the Sea of Galilee, which was known for ferocious storms that often erupted out of nowhere. The lead person on this boat wasn't George Clooney but Simon Peter, a disciple of Jesus. In all other respects, we can assume that the intensity of the wind and waves had the same effect on the disciples as it did on the fishermen in the movie—desperate loneliness in the face of extreme fear.

The passage says ominously, "The disciples were in trouble far away from land." These were professional fishermen and seasoned sailors. Scholars tell us that fishermen in that day were careful about venturing too far out on the Sea of Galilee, precisely because of sudden storms. All the same, these guys knew the territory. And they also knew enough to realize they were no match for the intensity of this storm. The Bible says, "A strong wind had arisen" and the fishermen were "fighting heavy waves." Now I love modern versions of the Bible, but sometimes the good ol' King James Version says it best. Here, the King James says, "The wind was contrary," suggesting this wasn't a normal storm. It was a storm with a mind of its own, an act of nature that seemed to have a contrary, even evil intent.

And so it's in the midst of this Galilean storm with a contrary spirit that the disciples find themselves alone and overwhelmed.

What storm are you facing? What storm in your life right now has a contrary spirit? What leaves you feeling all alone in the face of overwhelming obstacles? Is taming a storm the miracle you need today?

Three things converged to make this a perfect storm and terrify the disciples. These three things may have also converged in your life to create a perfect storm and perhaps fill you with fear.

STORM DAMAGE

"The disciples were in trouble far away from land." They had lost their bearings. *They had no sense of security.*

In a way we enter this story in the middle of act 2, the storm. Act 3 is Jesus walking on water, and act 4 is Jesus climbing into the boat. Where is act 1?

Act 1 happened before this passage begins. In the Bible this perfect storm comes right after Jesus fed the five thousand: "Immediately after this, Jesus insisted that his disciples get back into the boat and cross to the other side of the lake, while he sent the people home. After sending them home, he went up into the hills by himself to pray" (Matthew 14:22–23, NLT).

Act 1—the setup for the miracle of walking on water, the prologue to the perfect storm—is all about Jesus's sending the disciples out in a boat onto the Sea of Galilee. He knew He was sending them right into a storm. As we saw in the previous chapter, sometimes storms are part of God's plan for our lives. Sometimes a loss of security is part of God's plan for us because it's only then—when we have no bearings and no solid ground to step onto—that we have to depend on Him.

The Bible suggests that the disciples had *lost their stability*. "A strong wind had risen, and they were fighting heavy waves." There was no solid ground for them to stand on.

Even in calm seas a small boat feels shaky to my feet and legs. But fishermen are used to this, and the deck of a boat is, for them, firm ground. But the picture we have here is of a boat rocking wildly back and forth, much like the *Andrea Gail* in the movie. And in that situation even veteran fishermen have trouble keeping their legs under them.

Often life is like this. The things you have always counted on are no longer there. The people you thought supported you seem to have left you. The situations of life—a job, a career, the church—seem to be crumbling underneath your feet. Not only has major change come into your life, but it feels as if everything is changing all at once. This lack of stability, of certainty, about the ground underneath you can make you feel all alone in life.

The third face of loneliness is *the loss of visibility.* We all have had to drive in fog. Even when you're on a road you know well, one you've driven a hundred times, it's scary to drive it when you can't see anything clearly.

The Bible says the disciples found themselves in this contrary storm with winds blowing and waves crashing. The next sentence begins "about three o'clock in the morning." The boat's rocking and rolling, and it feels as if it's about to capsize, and it's the middle of the night, and the disciples can't see a thing.

Experts say that children's number-one fear is fear of the dark. What do children do when they're afraid of the dark? They look for a parent's hand to hold, or they run and jump into their parents' bed. Loss of visibility makes us feel alone, and we look for someone to take away our loneliness. When it seems our lives and futures have been plunged into the dark, we can feel just as fearful as kids. When a storm comes into our lives and we can't see what to do next, we may be filled with fear and feel very much alone in the dark.

When we find ourselves without security, stability, or visibility in life, we can be overwhelmed with fear and a sense of being all alone.

That's the bad news.

But—spoiler alert—in Christ the story ends well. Very well.

THE PRESENCE OF JESUS

You may have seen a YouTube video about a man named Derek Redmond. More than a million people watched the original video that was posted by the International Olympic Committee. Other copies of the video have been watched by a million more.

Redmond was a runner, a sprinter, on the British team that competed in the 1992 Summer Olympics in Barcelona. Derek specialized in the 400-meter sprint. Coming into the '92 Olympics, he was in top form and was favored to win the 400-meter race. He'd already won numerous races in the 4-x-400-meter relay. This was his solo moment.

In the first round Derek posted the fastest time of all the runners. He then won the quarterfinal and was at the starting blocks for the semifinal round.

All of this was caught on video. Wearing number 749, dressed in blue athletic shorts, and running in lane 5, Redmond settled into his stance moments before the starting gun went off.

He got off to a great start—perhaps the fastest out-of-the-blocks thrust he'd achieved in the Olympics. Heading into the turn, Derek was looking good. Some sixty-five thousand fans were cheering. And down the backstretch, Redmond appeared to be a shoo-in.

Then there was a pop. Derek said later he heard it and first thought it was the sound of a gun and that maybe someone had been shot. Then Derek felt the loss of strength in his right leg, then the pain. He started hopping. And then he fell onto the track on one knee, sobbing.

He knew then he'd just torn his hamstring. For a moment he leaned back onto the track, weeping, knowing his chance at a gold medal had just been derailed. And then Derek told himself that somehow he had to finish the race.

The video shows the incredible unfolding of the rest of the story.

Derek got up and started hopping slowly around the track. The race had finished, and the other runners had crossed the finish line. Despite the pain and disappointment, tears rolling down his cheeks, Derek willed himself to go on.

Suddenly the people in the stadium who had just cheered for one race became aware of another: a man fighting to finish the race despite injury and pain. The roar of the crowd grew louder as more spectators realized what Derek was trying to do. Despite a torn hamstring, this runner was continuing the race so he could finish.

In the stands an older man pushed aside security guards and made his way down toward the track.

Derek continued hopping on one leg, slowly inching his way to the finish line. The pain appeared excruciating. Could he make it?

The man from the stands pushed away another guard and ran onto the track. He yelled back at the security guards, "I'm going to help him." He came alongside the crippled runner and put his arm around Derek. The man was Derek's father.

This moment has made history. Few people remember the name Derek Redmond, but millions know how he vowed to keep going and how his father came alongside to help him finish the race.

"I'm here, Son," Jim Redmond said to his boy. "We'll finish together." Derek put his arm around his father's shoulders and leaned on his dad, sobbing, but still limping toward the finish.

A few steps from the end, the crowd cheering, Jim Redmond let go of his son so that Derek could cross the finish line by himself. Once Derek was across, Jim pulled his son into his embrace once again.

Speaking to the press later, Jim said with tears in his eyes, "I'm the proudest father alive. I'm prouder of him than I would have been if he had won the gold medal."[21]

I see a parallel to this miracle of Jesus walking on water.

We often look at this event as a lesson in faith. And, yes, there *is* a lesson of faith embedded here, and I will write about that too. But if we see this only as an instructional piece, one in which Jesus eventually chastises His disciples for their weak faith, we will miss the point.

I see this miracle as a picture of Jesus running onto the track to help His child finish the race. It's the image of Jesus walking into the midst of a storm to comfort His disciples in the midst of their aloneness and fear. It's the viral video of Jesus walking through the storm itself to reach the people He loves.

I can't think of many things more frightening than being on a boat in the middle of the night in a storm. A shaking, creaking boat on a dark, windy night, bobbing around on stormy black water would be terrifying.

And sometimes life is like that: dark, stormy, and scary.

The disciples were terrified, the Bible says. And in the midst of their terror, they saw a figure on the horizon, a mysterious being who was actually walking on the water!

The disciples thought this was a ghost. They didn't know it was Jesus. He'd waved good-bye to them from shore. And this was a violent storm in the middle of Nowhereville, Galilee. Remember the principle of the Miracle Map that says God does the miracle however He wants to do it, and it's usually in an unexpected way. The disciples absolutely never expected to see Jesus out there in the midst of the storm.

So often, neither do we.

We expect to experience God in church. We expect to experience God when we're reading our Bible and having our quiet time or our devotional. We expect to sense God's presence at funerals and prayer meetings. But we don't expect to experience God in a business downturn. We don't expect to experience God in the middle of marriage problems. We don't expect to experience God in the middle of our depression. We don't expect to experience God when we get sick.

Why is it that when our business downturn results in bankruptcy, when our marriage problems move us toward divorce, when our emotional blues turn into deep depression, when our sickness is diagnosed as a chronic illness—when we are suddenly faced with a big storm—we finally turn to God for help? Why do we fail to seek God in our problems but rush to Him when our problems push us to a point of desperation?

Why do we look for our miracle only when we are in the middle of a storm? Why not in the day to day of life? Why don't we ask God for a miracle all along?

I think it's because we are frail human beings. It's usually when I'm about to go under that I finally look to God and realize how much I need Him. When all is sunny and smooth sailing, we don't realize our great need for Him. We should. We should understand how fragile life is at every moment. God wants us to be connected with Him at all times. But our nature is such that, only when the storms hit and our fragile lives are beaten and battered, do we turn in desperation to God for help. Only when we feel the pain of loneliness, do we desperately reach for God.

In other words, we never receive a miracle until we realize we need a miracle.

I know some people read this passage and say the supernatural event occurred when Jesus walked on water. And that is an amazing thing. But I think we'd be wrong if we saw that as the only miracle here.

You see, the big miracle here wasn't *how* Jesus got to the boat. The big miracle was that Jesus showed up in the midst of a storm. And He will show up, I guarantee, in the middle of your lonely storm. You may experience Him walking on water, or maybe He will show up in some other way. That doesn't matter. What matters is that He will be there for you. Jesus will be there, walking onto the Olympic track of your life, coming alongside your labored, limping life, putting His arms around you, and saying, "I'm here, My son. I'm here, daughter of Mine. Take courage. We'll get to the finish line together. You are not alone."

JUMP OVERBOARD IN FAITH

Simon Peter has been criticized over the years for his brash personality, his denial of Christ on the morning of the crucifixion, and his impetuous actions. And he is often criticized for the lack of faith he showed in this account.

But I'd like to look at Peter's actions more closely. The passage says, "Peter called to him, 'Lord, if it's really you, tell me to come to you, walking on the water.' 'Yes, come,' Jesus said. So Peter went over the side of the boat."

Yes, I know there's more to come, and I know the next verse talks about Peter's faith faltering, but we'll get to that. For now let's focus on what happened first. And let me ask you a question: Would you have gotten out of the boat?

Remember the seas were churning, the winds were howling and contrary, and the boat was rocking from side to side. The disciples were terrified. And then a ghostlike figure appeared on the horizon, a figure that turned out to be Jesus walking on water. Would your first move be to go "over the side of the boat"?

That was Peter's first impulse.

A more rational approach might have been to yell to Jesus, "Come here! Get into the boat. Save us!" I would have stayed hunkered down in the boat, feeling a bit better now that Jesus was walking my way.

But Simon Peter got out of the boat. Let's give him credit.

We refer to this passage as the miracle of Jesus walking on water. We would do well to recognize this as also the miracle of *Peter* walking on water. He looked into the eyes of Jesus, and he was the only disciple—by faith—to get out of the boat! Sometimes you have to be willing to be the one to get out of the boat. There are times when you have to step out in faith, and no one else follows, and you feel all alone. That's when God grows your faith more than ever.

So with the other fishermen probably hunkered down in the boat as the perfect storm raged, Peter jumped over the side, looked across at Jesus, and stepped forward in faith. Peter was confronted with a divine moment. Not one that made him divine, of course, but a moment of encounter with the divine God through Jesus Christ.

Our first lesson from this miracle is that we need to *move forward in faith*. Sometimes that means to *jump overboard* in faith. Too often we wait for our fears to go away before we move forward. Often we stop to assess the pros and cons, do a pro forma report, and analyze our options. We tend to look for certainty in the midst of our troubles, for the rocks and boulders we can step on to keep us from falling into the water. But when we wait for certainty, we lose our chance at faith.

The feelings of fear won't go away, but when you step out in faith in spite of your fears, God blesses. Peter may have been afraid, but he didn't stop to calculate the odds of his success. Seeing a divine moment, Peter took his leap of faith.

I used to think that great men and women of God, the great heroes of the

Bible, never had any fears. Now I know that's not true. Everyone has fears. What the great heroes of the faith teach us is that God blesses when we take that leap of faith in spite of our fears.

My son Josh and his wife, Kelli, have been deepened spiritually by reading the works of the British preacher Charles Spurgeon. In fact, they've talked about Spurgeon at Woodlands Church, quoting his words from a devotional titled *Morning and Evening.* Spurgeon wrote, "You could not have belief in your own weakness had you not been compelled to pass through the rivers; and you would never have known God's strength had you not been supported amid the water-floods."[22] Josh commented on this in one of our church services, observing that "the most important thing about our faith is not just that we rejoice and praise God *in the midst of* hardship, but we rejoice and praise God *because of* hardship."

The storm you're facing right now may not be something you just need to survive. Very possibly the troubles in front of you are a remarkable opportunity for you to experience a great miracle.

You'll never find your miracle if you stay hunkered down in the boat.

EYES ON JESUS

Peter's example is so helpful to us. He jumped overboard in faith, started walking on water, and then took his focus off Jesus.

I read this and think, *That's so totally me.* Don't you love the character of Peter? Don't you love that he's in the Bible and that he's like you and me?

The passage tells us, "But when he saw the strong wind and the waves, he was terrified and began to sink." In other words, when Peter looked past the storm into the eyes of Christ, God gave him the power to walk on the water. But when Peter looked at the stormy circumstances around him, the wind and the waves, he became fearful and started to go under. When Peter looked at the waves, he forgot about Jesus and felt like he was all alone in the storm.

I imagine you've heard this lesson from this miracle before. But I think this simple teaching has another layer of meaning. When we look at Jesus, we see reflected in His eyes an image of ourselves, our true worth, our real value. Our faith in Him yields a confidence in *who we are in Him.* When we are looking to find our miracle and we look into the eyes of Jesus, we see ourselves as He sees us—beloved, cherished, and worthy.

But when we look away, when we see the circumstances that surround us, when we see the waves of problems we face, when we no longer see our reflection in Jesus's eyes, suddenly we question who we are, what we can do, and if we can overcome. We lose faith in the miracle that God may have for us, because our view of the world no longer has Christ in it.

Maybe you're looking around at the waves that are crashing against you, and it feels as if you're all alone. No. The God of the universe is with you. It's just that you lost your focus on Jesus. You focused on the fear and stopped looking at the One who loves you with His life.

Here's a simpler way to say it: When we look at ourselves, we become overwhelmed by our powerlessness. When we look at Jesus, we become empowered to jump overboard into the miracle He has for us.

It's no accident that so many songs and hymns speak about our seeing Jesus, looking toward Him, and fixing our eyes on Him. "Turn Your Eyes upon Jesus," "Be Thou My Vision," and "Open My Eyes That I May See" all call us to look into the eyes of Jesus and see our circumstances in the context of the great Miracle Worker.

As you seek your miracle, remember Peter walking on water as he looked into Jesus's eyes. Peter was doing fine until he looked away from Jesus and became overwhelmed by his circumstances.

Remember this lesson: *focus on Jesus.* Don't focus on the perfect storm that's in your life. Focus on the perfect love of your Savior that will never let you go.

He didn't bring you this far to let you drown.

CRY OUT TO GOD

The Bible reports that Peter cried out, "Save me, Lord!"

We assume he was yelling. But regardless of the volume, I consider this a prayer.

It's a prayer of fear. It's a prayer of need. It's a prayer of confession: "I can't do this on my own, Lord!"

This may be the shortest prayer in the Bible. I think it is also the most often uttered prayer of all time. Throughout the Bible and all of history, human beings have time and time again come to the end of their rope and cried out, "Save me, God!"

One of the Miracle Map principles is that miracles often happen when you're at the end of your rope. We see that here—except that Peter had no literal rope to hang on to, no nautical line to take hold of, no mast rigging to grab for safety. He had only Jesus in front of him as he was sinking.

Peter prayed in a loud voice that cut through the roar of the storm, "Save me, Lord!" I think that God works miracles when we cry out in desperation to Him. That night Peter discovered the power of his desperate cry. Jesus saved him as he was slipping into the water.

The cry of desperate faith will always be heard by God.

A strange but true story hit the news in 2015. Four policemen arrived at the scene of an accident and heard a woman crying for help from an upside-down car partially submerged in the river.

They rushed into the forty-degree water and pushed the car over. Peering inside, they found an eighteen-month-old child still alive and harnessed in her car seat, which hung just above the water. However, the mother, in the driver's seat, had been killed. It was later determined that she had died on impact, fourteen hours earlier.

Yet all four officers heard an adult voice coming from the car.[23]

There has been no explanation for this strange occurrence. Is there a natural explanation? Perhaps. Is it a miracle? I believe it could be. We may never know. But because I believe in miracles, I believe it could be that a miracle saved a baby girl that day.

I truly believe it's possible that God allowed this mother's voice to be heard from beyond death to save her little girl. And I believe such a cry, a prayer of desperation, is powerful in our lives as well.

The Bible says, "Jesus immediately reached out and grabbed [Peter]." Peter prayed a prayer, a call for help, and Jesus grabbed him.

When, in the face of fear, you cry for help, whether you shout or whisper a prayer to God for deliverance, God is there to work a miracle. I believe He will grab you out of the troubled waters below.

WORSHIP THE GOD OF ALL MIRACLES

So what happened at the end of this miracle within a miracle within a miracle? The Bible reports this in act 4:

> "You have so little faith," Jesus said. "Why did you doubt me?"
> When [Jesus and Peter] climbed back into the boat, the wind stopped. Then the disciples worshiped him. "You really are the Son of God!" they exclaimed.

I think sometimes we read these words of Jesus—"You have so little faith" and "Why did you doubt me?"—as if they had a judgmental tone. I'm not so sure. I think it's possible Jesus spoke with a tone of comfort: "Guys, I had your backs all along. You should know Me better than that. Relax. I've got this."

Or maybe Jesus's intent here was essentially to say, "Gentlemen, do I have to connect all the dots for you? You've seen Me heal the lame and sick, you experienced one morning the greatest fish catch you'd ever seen, and just yesterday you watched Me feed five thousand people with a few loaves and fish. Don't you believe I can handle some stormy weather?"

I think Jesus may have been simply observing that His disciples, amazed as they were by the many miracles He had done so far, still didn't understand or accept *who Jesus was*. What happened next directly led to that deeper understanding in the hearts of the fishermen.

This story that started with a ferocious storm, with the wind howling and contrary, finds Jesus walking back to the boat on the water with Peter. But He was speaking to all the disciples: "Don't you yet know what I can do?"

Then the storm stopped.

It just stopped. In Luke's account of a similar miracle, he reported that Jesus "rebuked the wind and the raging waves." And "suddenly the storm stopped and all was calm" (8:24, NLT). There's that word again—*suddenly*.

Amazing. So this Jesus has power over nature. The disciples, Luke wrote, asked themselves a question: "Who is this man? . . . Even the wind and waves obey him!" (8:25, NLT). Their eyes were opening to see God Himself. The God outside of nature had entered into nature and, as "supernature," had changed everything.

In Matthew we are told, "The disciples worshiped him."

This is a miracle that keeps on giving. We first read that Jesus walked on water. Then we realize that the real miracle here was the presence of Jesus in the midst of a storm. Then we learn that Peter "went over the side of the boat *and walked on the water* toward Jesus." Then we watch as Jesus controls nature itself.

But the ultimate miracle here is something more. No, This miracle isn't really about water and waves. It's not about a boat in a storm. It's not even about walking on water, although God will provide the miracle you need and, in one way or another, will enable you to walk on water.

This miracle is about *a full, deep realization of who Jesus is*. "You really are the Son of God!" the disciples exclaimed. Remember the fourth principle of the

Miracle Map? *A miracle of God will always bring glory to God and point people to Jesus.*

Ultimately the miracle in your life is about your deeper understanding of who Jesus is.

Come to grips with the knowledge of who He is, understand that He is present with you in your life right now and always—you are not alone!—and then kneel and worship the absolutely astonishing living God who will never leave you or forsake you.

Promises for When You're Lonely

The Lord will not abandon his people, because that would dishonor his great name. For it has pleased the Lord to make you his very own people.

1 Samuel 12:22, NLT

Even if my father and mother abandon me,
>   the Lord will hold me close.

Psalm 27:10, NLT

A hostile world! I call to God,
>   I cry to God to help me.
From his palace he hears my call;
>   my cry brings me right into his presence—
>   a private audience!

Psalm 18:6, MSG

A father to the fatherless, a defender of widows,
>   is God in his holy dwelling.
God sets the lonely in families,
>   he leads out the prisoners with singing;
>   but the rebellious live in a sun-scorched land.

Psalm 68:5–6

"Though the mountains be shaken
>   and the hills be removed,

yet my unfailing love for you will not be shaken
    nor my covenant of peace be removed,"
    says the LORD, who has compassion on you.

        Isaiah 54:10

One who has unreliable friends soon comes to ruin,
    but there is a friend who sticks closer than a brother.

        Proverbs 18:24

Be strong and courageous. Do not be afraid or terrified because of them, for the LORD your God goes with you; he will never leave you nor forsake you.

        Deuteronomy 31:6

Jesus: The Life Giver

The birth, death, and resurrection of Jesus means that one day everything sad will come untrue.

—J. R. R. Tolkien

Miracles are a retelling in small letters of the very same story which is written across the whole world in letters too large for some of us to see.

—C. S. Lewis

10

When You're Hurting

Jesus Raises Lazarus

Now a man named Lazarus was sick. He was from
Bethany, the village of Mary and her sister Martha. (This
Mary, whose brother Lazarus now lay sick, was the same
one who poured perfume on the Lord and wiped his feet
with her hair.) So the sisters sent word to Jesus, "Lord, the
one you love is sick."

When he heard this, Jesus said, "This sickness will not
end in death. No, it is for God's glory so that God's Son
may be glorified through it." Now Jesus loved Martha and
her sister and Lazarus. So when he heard that Lazarus was
sick, he stayed where he was two more days, and then he
said to his disciples, "Let us go back to Judea."

"But Rabbi," they said, "a short while ago the Jews
there tried to stone you, and yet you are going back?"

Jesus answered, "Are there not twelve hours of daylight? Anyone who walks in the daytime will not stumble,
for they see by this world's light. It is when a person walks
at night that they stumble, for they have no light."

After he had said this, he went on to tell them, "Our

friend Lazarus has fallen asleep; but I am going there to wake him up."

His disciples replied, "Lord, if he sleeps, he will get better." Jesus had been speaking of his death, but his disciples thought he meant natural sleep.

So then he told them plainly, "Lazarus is dead, and for your sake I am glad I was not there, so that you may believe. But let us go to him."

Then Thomas (also known as Didymus) said to the rest of the disciples, "Let us also go, that we may die with him."

On his arrival, Jesus found that Lazarus had already been in the tomb for four days. Now Bethany was less than two miles from Jerusalem, and many Jews had come to Martha and Mary to comfort them in the loss of their brother. When Martha heard that Jesus was coming, she went out to meet him, but Mary stayed at home.

"Lord," Martha said to Jesus, "if you had been here, my brother would not have died. But I know that even now God will give you whatever you ask."

Jesus said to her, "Your brother will rise again."

Martha answered, "I know he will rise again in the resurrection at the last day."

Jesus said to her, "I am the resurrection and the life. The one who believes in me will live, even though they die; and whoever lives by believing in me will never die. Do you believe this?"

"Yes, Lord," she replied, "I believe that you are the Messiah, the Son of God, who is to come into the world."

After she had said this, she went back and called her

sister Mary aside. "The Teacher is here," she said, "and is asking for you." When Mary heard this, she got up quickly and went to him. Now Jesus had not yet entered the village, but was still at the place where Martha had met him. When the Jews who had been with Mary in the house, comforting her, noticed how quickly she got up and went out, they followed her, supposing she was going to the tomb to mourn there.

When Mary reached the place where Jesus was and saw him, she fell at his feet and said, "Lord, if you had been here, my brother would not have died."

When Jesus saw her weeping, and the Jews who had come along with her also weeping, he was deeply moved in spirit and troubled. "Where have you laid him?" he asked.

"Come and see, Lord," they replied.

Jesus wept.

Then the Jews said, "See how he loved him!"

But some of them said, "Could not he who opened the eyes of the blind man have kept this man from dying?"

Jesus, once more deeply moved, came to the tomb. It was a cave with a stone laid across the entrance. "Take away the stone," he said.

"But, Lord," said Martha, the sister of the dead man, "by this time there is a bad odor, for he has been there four days."

Then Jesus said, "Did I not tell you that if you believe, you will see the glory of God?"

So they took away the stone. Then Jesus looked up and said, "Father, I thank you that you have heard me. I knew that you always hear me, but I said this for the benefit of the people standing here, that they may believe that you sent me."

When he had said this, Jesus called in a loud voice, "Lazarus, come out!" The dead man came out, his hands and feet wrapped with strips of linen, and a cloth around his face.

Jesus said to them, "Take off the grave clothes and let him go."

—John 11:1–44

"SHE WAS CLINICALLY DEAD," Dr. Ford stated. "They had called the code and pronounced her dead."

Connie Davis had been rushed to the hospital with a pulmonary embolism. For two hours medics performed CPR. They waited. Still nothing.

They called the code. They pronounced Connie Davis dead.

What doctors and nurses didn't know was that a small army of prayer warriors at the Davises' church were storming heaven for a miracle. What the prayer group didn't know was that Connie was already dead.

The family came into the hospital room. Gathering around to pray, her husband, Tommy, took her hand, which was cold. And then, a slight squeeze.

Life, miraculously, was coming back into Connie's body.

Doctors and nurses rushed back to the room. Just fifteen hours after she had been pronounced dead, Connie Davis was, incredibly, able to write a note to her husband. She asked him to cancel an appointment.

Thirty days later she was discharged from the hospital. She made a full recovery. She said she prayed, "Father, if You don't really need me, I'd really like to raise my son."[24]

A Greater Miracle

There are other stories like Connie Davis's—true, verified accounts of people pronounced dead who came back to life. Many doctors and nurses have seen events like this they can't explain. Maybe you know of someone who has experienced death yet is alive. Such things do happen, and I believe they are miracles of death being overcome, even in this modern day and time.

But these stories are amazing to us because they are rare. We know that death is inevitable. We all will die sometime. We all acknowledge the power of death. And it's something that many—maybe most of us—fear.

We live in death's shadow. We are constantly concerned about what bad things might happen. We try to protect ourselves and loved ones against possible tragedy. And we hope and pray we can stay free of terminal illness. In many ways physical death defines a lot of life.

So when death *is* overcome, that miracle fills us with awe and perhaps a measure of hope. We glimpse for real what we know by faith—that there is a power greater than death.

This is the context for the great, profound miracle in which Jesus brought His close friend Lazarus back to life.

This was not, however, the first time Jesus raised someone from the dead. The Bible reports that Jesus brought back to life a widow's son who was being taken out of town to be buried (see Luke 7:13–15) and raised the daughter of a synagogue leader named Jairus (see Matthew 9:18–26).

But the story of Lazarus is different. In many ways the raising of Lazarus was a miracle that topped every other miracle Jesus had done at that point. And I suggest it's significant because this miracle was more *public,* more *timely,* and much more *personal* than other miracles Jesus performed.

It's helpful to know that the small village of Bethany, where Lazarus had lived, was just a mile and a half from Jerusalem, a populous city and the seat of religious and political government. News of whatever Jesus did in Bethany would be quickly carried down the street into the big city. His actions would soon be very *public*. What happened in Bethany would not stay in Bethany.

We know now what the disciples did not know then: within weeks of this miracle, Jesus would be riding on a donkey, along that same street, into Jerusalem in what we know as the Triumphal Entry—the event we celebrate on Palm Sunday. Then one week after that, Jesus would be tried, sentenced, and crucified. In fact, this miracle of Lazarus created big-time publicity among the immense crowds following Him and among the religious leaders in Jerusalem, who weren't, to say the least, big fans. So the *timing* of this miracle was no accident. Jesus's raising Lazarus from the dead became one of the catalysts leading to Jesus's death.

The very special relationship of Jesus with Mary and Martha and Lazarus also made this one different. This was *personal*. These verses in John 11 show that Jesus was very close to Mary, Martha, and Lazarus. Several Bible passages refer to Jesus visiting them in Bethany, sharing meals with them, and having conversations with them. The well-known account of Mary sitting at Jesus's feet while Martha prepared dinner is an intimate picture of Jesus in a home. Some scholars surmise this was a frequent stop for Jesus. It's clear that these three siblings were close friends of Jesus, He enjoyed their company, and He cared about them deeply in a *personal* way.

For all these reasons—its public presence, its timely occurrence, and its personal aspect—the miracle of raising Lazarus was part of Jesus's ministry for a specific purpose. It is the miracle that seals the deal about who Jesus is. It is the miracle that sets in motion the final events of Jesus's life on earth. And it is the crowning triumph of the supernatural over the natural.

GOD IS NEVER LATE

Lazarus was sick. Gravely sick. The two sisters, Mary and Martha, sent word to Jesus. They knew Jesus healed the sick, and they expected Him to rush to Bethany to heal His close friend.

Most scholars believe Jesus and His disciples were in a southern town only one day's traveling distance from Bethany when He received the news that Lazarus was sick. The Bible tells us that Jesus "stayed where he was two more days" after He was told that His friend was gravely ill.

So Jesus *chose to wait* and let His friend Lazarus die. Of course that prompts all sorts of questions: Did He really care about Lazarus? Did He care about Mary and Martha?

Immediately, I think about the third principle in the Miracle Map: God does the miracle in His way and in *His time.* God's miracles are never late, and they are never early. They come to us right on time. It just doesn't seem like it to us. We can't see the big picture, and many times it feels as if God is running late or He's completely forgotten about us.

Mary and Martha felt that Jesus was two days late, but Jesus knew He was right on time. Jesus was following the divine plan, and He knew the plan wasn't to heal a sick man. No, the plan was to raise a dead man and show that Jesus is the Life Giver.

I think it is obvious this miracle was specially and divinely orchestrated to be of great significance. I think it is less obvious how agonizing this must have been for Jesus—to sit and wait as His close friend Lazarus died and to stay away from the sisters, whom He clearly loved. We might get so caught up in the mechanics of this miracle that we overlook the emotion Jesus felt. This is one of the times that the story of Jesus shows the tension within Him between His divinity and His humanity. Jesus was God, fully divine, and these circumstances had to align in a certain way so the glory of God could be revealed perfectly. Jesus was also a man, fully human, and this experience—the death of a friend— was real and personal to Him, just as it was to Mary and Martha and everyone else around Him.

After two days Jesus said to His disciples that it was time to go to Judea. They warned Him of the dangers. Previously, Bethany had been a rough part of town for Jesus and the disciples. They'd nearly been stoned there once before.

Jesus responded to the disciples' concern with this cryptic, fascinating statement: "Are there not twelve hours of daylight? Anyone who walks in the daytime will not stumble, for they see by this world's light. It is when a person walks at night that they stumble, for they have no light."

What? What is this about?

I think Jesus—here and later in this account—was pointing everyone to consider the larger picture of God's purposes and His kingdom. Jesus was saying, yes, there is the reality of the world we live in—the light of daytime, the dangers of violence in a southern town, and the physical reality of death. But Jesus might have been implying there's another kind of light to live by. The words here echo the opening of Psalm 27: "The LORD is my light and my salvation—whom shall I fear? The LORD is the stronghold of my life—of whom shall I be afraid?"

In these moments of Jesus's life, He was walking into the twilight of His ministry on earth. Neither the disciples nor Lazarus nor Mary and Martha could have known this. But Jesus knew what was ahead for Him—and for all humanity. All His preaching and teaching and speaking to crowds from hillsides and boats about the kingdom of God now was becoming more urgent. Indeed the kingdom of Light and the world of darkness were about to collide in an event that would change everything.

In these words about daylight and night, Jesus was saying that there is this present world with its light of day and dark nights, but there is also the kingdom of God and the light of God's Word. He was saying that in a short while the normal definitions of light and dark wouldn't apply anymore.

Jesus went on to tell His disciples that Lazarus had "fallen asleep." They responded as if Jesus were talking about nighttime sleep, but Jesus was referring to death. He came out directly and said, "Lazarus is dead."

So not only was Jesus saying the usual understanding of light and dark didn't apply anymore, but the usual understanding of *death* didn't apply anymore either.

As strange and cryptic as Jesus's words are, I think there's a very clear lesson in them for you and me.

As you seek your miracle today, you may be going through a dark time. Life is filled with dark times, but perhaps the situation you're in feels like one of the darkest. No doubt Mary and Martha felt this as well. Their brother Lazarus was dying. They, too, were seeking their miracle.

But like them, perhaps you, too, need to have a better sense of how God's kingdom works. In His kingdom, darkness is not darkness. In His kingdom, sickness is not sickness.

And in His kingdom, death is not death.

THE SOURCE OF MIRACLES IS THE MESSIAH

And so Jesus finally went to Bethany.

Talk about a hopeless mission. He was going to a place where He was likely to be assaulted, and He was going to heal a man who had just died. What's more, Jesus had to face Mary and Martha's hurt and disappointment that He had not arrived in time to save their brother.

The biblical account tells us Martha went out to meet Jesus, but Mary stayed home. This is interesting. Remember the earlier story of Jesus visiting Mary and Martha in their home? Martha was the one working in the kitchen to make the meal, and she was frustrated with Mary, who sat at Jesus's feet rather than helping her. Jesus had reprimanded Martha for focusing on things that were less significant. Mary was the one who valued her face time with her Lord.

But here it was *Martha* running out to Jesus. We don't know for sure, but it seems important to the writer of this gospel to report that Mary stayed home. Perhaps Mary was so upset Jesus hadn't arrived in time that she couldn't bear to see Him. Maybe she was deep in her grief over Lazarus and deep in her anger at Jesus.

Maybe you're going through a season of deep hurt. The loss of a loved one.

The pain of divorce. A close friend's betrayal. Sometimes when we're hurting and bleeding on the inside, we have trouble talking to God. At times the pain is so great that no words can express it. The great news is that in those darkest moments when we don't feel like bringing our hurts to Christ, Christ comes to us anyway.

Martha was now the one, it seems, whose understanding about Jesus had grown. She ran to him and said, "Jesus, we're disappointed that You didn't come at once. If You'd been here, my brother wouldn't have died." Martha stated the sisters' frustration with Jesus. But then she said something that revealed her great faith: "Even now God will give you whatever you ask." Martha seemed to know it was not too late.

Jesus said to Martha, "Your brother will rise again."

Martha, remembering well the teaching of her friend and Lord, replied, "I know he will rise again in the resurrection at the last day."

And once again we have this strange language that speaks of the intersection of the now and the not yet, of earth and heaven, of life temporal and life eternal, of the physical invaded by the supernatural, of death but then life. Jesus says some of the most extraordinary words in all of Scripture: "I am the resurrection and the life. The one who believes in me will live, even though they die; and whoever lives by believing in me will never die."

And this language, these cryptic words, brought a moment of crystal clarity to one human being who utterly, absolutely *got it*. Martha said, "I believe that you are the Messiah, the Son of God, who is to come into the world."

As I have noted before, so many of Jesus's miracles point to this central question of who He is. And time and time again, as the Miracle Map suggests, the miracle brings us closer to the person of Christ.

Here lies the great hope for you and me as people who seek our miracle. If the miracles of Jesus up to now merely suggested or implied something about His identity, about who He truly is, this miracle finally nailed it. Jesus is indeed the Son of God, the Messiah, living, breathing, and oh so amazingly working among us.

Jesus is the way, the truth, and the LIFE!

JESUS THE COMFORTER

Jesus asked Martha to get Mary. There is a great tenderness in this—Jesus engaging with Martha first of all and then asking for her sister, no doubt knowing how deep in pain Mary was.

"Jesus is asking for you," Martha told her sister.

Can you imagine anything better than that? Anything more soul-touching than those words? And yet it's true for you too: *Jesus is asking for you.* In all those down times of your life—those phases when you're away from God, those situations in which you are hurting, crying, grieving—Jesus is aware that you are sitting apart in your pain. He notices you aren't near. He knows the agony you're in. And then He asks for you.

Isn't that a wonderful thing? Isn't that amazing? He wants to see you. He knows you are hurting, and He wants to be with you. Jesus is asking for you.

Mary heard her sister, got up, and ran to Jesus. As I said, I think Mary was filled with grief over her brother's death and also anger at Jesus for not being there before Lazarus died. I think that because it would be so human, so normal, so like you and me. We, too, are Marys.

Some people are angry at God. I know I have been. Maybe you're angry at God for not healing someone in your life, for not fixing a mess that's developed, for not intervening to prevent a set of circumstances. And it's okay to be angry at God. In fact, the Bible shows us people, like Jonah, who were angry at Him and yet ultimately were blessed by God and became a great blessing to others.

Let's face it. Whenever we're angry at someone for hurting us or whenever we're angry about the problems in our lives that we didn't cause, who are we really angry at? God. God doesn't cause evil, and God doesn't cause someone to hurt you deeply, but He is all-powerful, and He could have stopped it.

But the Lord knows that our finite minds can never grasp here on this earth His eternal and purposeful plan. There are times when I don't understand at all what God is up to in my life. There are times when I see someone go through a terrible tragedy, and it makes no sense to me. There are times when I get angry at God.

And I know that in those times God wants us to come to Him with our anger, confusion, tears, and pain. Sometimes I don't want to admit that I am angry at God, because that doesn't seem a very spiritual response to my Lord. The truth is, God already knows when I'm mad at Him. I can't hide anything from God.

God's not going to punish you or strike you with a bolt of lightning when you bring your anger and frustration to Him. He loves you, and His heart is breaking with yours. When you're hurting, you can scream at God. You can cry out to God. You can weep in front of God. You can pour out all your questions before God. The only thing you can't afford to do is try to hide your hurt from God and stop talking to Him.

Just as He did for Mary, however, God will still call to you even when you try to hide your hurt from Him.

GOD CRIES

Throughout this entire miracle, you can't help but be aware of the great depth of emotions depicted here. The death of a friend, the anger of a sister, the grieving of a family—it's the stuff of great tragedy, Shakespearean drama, and grand opera.

Mary ran to Jesus and fell at His feet in tears. Through her tears she said, "Lord, if you had been here, my brother would not have died." These are the exact words her sister had spoken to Jesus. It suggests the two sisters had talked about this extensively, that Jesus's delay was a matter of conversation between them, and that they'd used these same words with each other as they had talked about Jesus.

Some people followed Mary to where Jesus was, and they were weeping too. The Bible says that Jesus "was deeply moved in spirit and troubled."

And it is here we encounter the short, simple sentence that is the subject of great analysis by scholars: "Jesus wept." Some argue that His tears were because of the unbelief of the people there. Others believe that Jesus was angry at death itself and wept that it has such power and control over the human race.

But I understand these two words to mean what seems most obvious: Jesus was weeping alongside those people He loved. He shared their grief, experienced their loss, and felt the agony they were feeling deep inside. The fact that Jesus is God and could—and did—raise Lazarus from the dead a few moments later did not keep Jesus from feeling the emotional pain His friends were suffering. I think Jesus was crying because His friends Mary and Martha were hurting so very much.

I wonder, as you seek your miracle, if you truly understand this. As you look to the divine God for a miraculous deliverance, do you overlook the depth of Jesus's love, the agony He feels *with you* in your situation?

One friend had died, two other close friends were grieving, and His disciples were whispering in His ear that Bethany was a dangerous place to be. Jesus, as God, could and would navigate all of this and make things right. But Jesus, as a man, felt deeply the emotional pain His friends carried. He cried too. His heart was broken too. He wept just as they wept.

And Jesus shares in the hurt, the pain, the grief that you are experiencing right now.

Yes, I believe that God can work a real, true-blue miracle in your life. I pray that He will. But in reaching for the miracle God can provide, don't miss the miracle God *has already* provided—the miracle of Jesus's presence, the Son of God who is right here beside you.

JESUS THE CONQUEROR

Jesus asked to be taken to the place Lazarus was buried.

Meanwhile, there was a buzz in the crowd. Some, seeing Jesus's tears, whispered about how much He loved Lazarus. But others were critical, saying that since this Jesus had healed others—opening the eyes of a blind man, for example—He certainly could have saved the life of Lazarus if only He had gotten there sooner.

I wonder if Jesus got tired of this throughout His ministry. People not believing, then seeing a miracle, then criticizing Him for performing the miracle on the Sabbath or not performing a miracle or, in this case, for not getting to a man's deathbed on time.

God gives us so much, yet how often are we disappointed?

Here, Jesus shrugged off the negative comments and walked to the tomb of Lazarus. He instructed others to move the stone away. Martha assumed that Jesus wanted to go into the tomb to be close to Lazarus and grieve in his presence, but she warned her Lord that the body had been there for four days and there would be a terribly bad odor. Pragmatic Martha, now wishing she had a can of Febreze.

Jesus spoke to her again about seeing the glory of God.

And then, in the presence of His critics, some unbelievers, and the naysayers chirping about His failure to get there sooner, Jesus commanded Lazarus to come forth. And in front of this crowd, the dead man, Lazarus, walked out of the tomb, still wrapped in graveclothes.

Miracle done.

Take that, naysayers!

One word of advice for those of us who are seeking to find our personal miracle: *Don't ever underestimate the miracle power of Jesus Christ, the Son of God.* Don't count Him out. Don't give up on God. As you're waiting for a miracle to happen, don't think that He has shown up too late. Nothing in your life is beyond the power of God.

But I would steer you wrong if I said that the Lazarus miracle was ultimately a way for Jesus to get back at His critics. It was not that. It was something else. Something much, much more.

What Jesus did here was nothing less than *overcome death itself.* Death has been a plague on humanity since the Garden of Eden. Through millenniums, through all of biblical history, human beings have struggled, fought, and even committed crimes to avoid the agony of death. And here, on a public stage in the presence of His enemies, Jesus delivered a perfect uppercut, a stunning punch to the chin of the Prince of Death. Death does *not* rule this earth. Death is not the end. That Jesus—see what He did here? "Yea, though I walk through the valley of the shadow of death, I will fear no evil" (Psalm 23:4, KJV). Those words are not just lines in a poem. They are now a reality.

What Jesus did here was nothing less than *entirely redefine death.* This miracle was a game changer. To God there is death and then there is Death. There is physical death, which is not the end and is not beyond the power of the supernatural God. But there is something more important than physical death. What exists beyond is spiritual Life and spiritual Death. Suddenly all that cryptic language Jesus used before becomes clear: "I am the resurrection and the life. The one who believes in me will live, even though they die; and whoever lives by believing in me will never die." In Christ, we are saved from spiritual Death. Physical death is not the issue or the problem.

THE COMING ATTRACTION

And what Jesus did in this miracle of raising Lazarus from the dead was to point to His own death and resurrection. This story foreshadows what was to come in a matter of weeks just down the street in Jerusalem. Lazarus is the preview to the feature film *Jesus Resurrected.*

Is deliverance from death the miracle you need to find today? Is your friend or parent, your sibling or child facing a difficult chronic illness? Are you dealing with a stunning diagnosis and difficult prognosis for yourself?

My heart goes out to you. These are hard things. But I truly believe this miracle of Lazarus can speak to you in a special way and tell you a number of things that are precisely what you need in these moments.

It tells you that if you think Jesus is showing up late, you might want to be careful about underestimating His purposes and power. I know so often you pray and pray and pray for a miracle to happen. And, yes, you believe that miracles do happen, that God works miracles, back then and still today. But sometimes God doesn't work a miracle; sometimes nothing happens. You are left wondering why He didn't show up. Yes, that's hard to swallow, especially when the current picture is dim and dark. But, quite simply, your timing may not be God's timing. He may not give you the miracle you want when you want it. God will work His will as He wills it, when He wills it. So when you feel God is not responding, choose the faith of Martha, and embrace who Jesus truly is: "You are the Messiah, the Son of God, who is to come into the world." Say it out loud. Pray that out loud. Shout it out loud. Know that God Himself is there with you, as Jesus was with Martha and Mary in Bethany, and know that His timing is perfect and purposeful—whatever that might mean in your circumstances.

This miracle tells you that Jesus is weeping with you right now. He feels the heartache, the grief, the fear, the pain, and the loss you feel. He really does. The Bible says, "He took up our infirmities and bore our diseases" (Matthew 8:17). The death of Lazarus that He overcame would be, in short time, the death He would endure and overcome. Know that Jesus stands alongside you and bears the weight of your situation.

The Lazarus miracle tells you that Jesus is your Comforter whatever you're facing right now. Isaiah called Jesus the "Wonderful Counselor" (9:6). He is there to weep with you and to comfort you, as He did with Mary and Martha. Talk to Him. Listen to Him.

And the miracle of Lazarus being raised tells you that Jesus has conquered death. As Paul wrote, "O death, where is your victory? O death, where is your sting?" (1 Corinthians 15:55, ESV). Death is not an end but a beginning. Physical death does not put a stop to eternal life. There is more. And the more is better.

Ultimately, the story of Lazarus was but a taste of what was to come. Jesus had entered the lives of Lazarus, Mary, and Martha, and He had performed a great miracle that showed His power over death. But that was only a foreshadowing of what He Himself would soon face.

Jesus, the Son of God, was just getting started. In a matter of weeks He would remove the sting of death once and for all and accomplish not only His resurrection but guarantee yours as well.

Promises for When You're Hurting

You've kept track of my every toss and turn
    through the sleepless nights,
Each tear entered in your ledger,
    each ache written in your book.

Psalm 56:8, MSG

For his anger lasts only a moment,
    but his favor lasts a lifetime!
Weeping may last through the night,
    but joy comes with the morning.

Psalm 30:5, NLT

I have told you all this so that you may have peace in me. Here on earth you will have many trials and sorrows. But take heart, because I have overcome the world.

John 16:33, NLT

And He who sits on the throne said, "Behold, I am making all things new." And He said, "Write, for these words are faithful and true."

Revelation 21:5, NASB

I remain confident of this:
    I will see the goodness of the Lord
    in the land of the living.

Wait for the LORD;

be strong and take heart

and wait for the LORD.

Psalm 27:13–14

Praise be to the God and Father of our Lord Jesus Christ, the Father of compassion and the God of all comfort, who comforts us in all our troubles, so that we can comfort those in any trouble with the comfort we ourselves receive from God.

2 Corinthians 1:3–4

When Jesus therefore saw his mother, and the disciple standing by, whom he loved, he saith unto his mother, Woman, behold thy son!

John 19:26, KJV

11

When You've Given Up

The Resurrection of Jesus

And when the centurion, who stood there in front of Jesus, saw how he died, he said, "Surely this man was the Son of God!"

—Mark 15:39

Now Thomas (also known as Didymus), one of the Twelve, was not with the disciples when Jesus came. So the other disciples told him, "We have seen the Lord!"

But he said to them, "Unless I see the nail marks in his hands and put my finger where the nails were, and put my hand into his side, I will not believe."

A week later his disciples were in the house again, and Thomas was with them. Though the doors were locked, Jesus came and stood among them and said, "Peace be with you!" Then he said to Thomas, "Put your finger here; see my hands. Reach out your hand and put it into my side. Stop doubting and believe."

Thomas said to him, "My Lord and my God!"

Then Jesus told him, "Because you have seen me, you

have believed; blessed are those who have not seen and yet have believed."

—John 20:24–29

Now Mary stood outside the tomb crying. As she wept, she bent over to look into the tomb and saw two angels in white, seated where Jesus' body had been, one at the head and the other at the foot.

They asked her, "Woman, why are you crying?"

"They have taken my Lord away," she said, "and I don't know where they have put him." At this, she turned around and saw Jesus standing there, but she did not realize that it was Jesus.

He asked her, "Woman, why are you crying? Who is it you are looking for?"

Thinking he was the gardener, she said, "Sir, if you have carried him away, tell me where you have put him, and I will get him."

Jesus said to her, "Mary."

She turned toward him and cried out in Aramaic, "Rabboni!" (which means "Teacher").

Jesus said, "Do not hold on to me, for I have not yet ascended to the Father. Go instead to my brothers and tell them, 'I am ascending to my Father and your Father, to my God and your God.'"

Mary Magdalene went to the disciples with the news: "I have seen the Lord!" And she told them that he had said these things to her.

—John 20:11–18

C. S. LEWIS CALLED THE INCARNATION—the birth, life, death, and resurrection of Jesus Christ—the "Grand Miracle," the superlative event that makes all other miracles possible and gives them meaning. He wrote, "All the well-established Christian miracles are part of [the Incarnation], that they all either prepare for, or exhibit, or result from the Incarnation."[25]

Lewis wrote about those who try to "strip Christianity" of its "miraculous elements" and those who suggest Christianity would be a "less embarrassing" religion if people didn't have to believe in supernatural events—in particular, the crazy notion that Jesus rose from the dead. Lewis said, "The Christian story is precisely the story of one grand miracle . . . what is beyond all space and time, which is uncreated, eternal, came into Nature, into human nature, descended into his own universe, and rose again, bringing Nature up with him. . . . If you take that away there is nothing specifically Christian left."[26] Indeed, the Resurrection is the linchpin for Christianity, and any miracle that might happen today is only possible because of Jesus's death and resurrection.

The miracle you seek for your life today depends utterly and completely on the life, death, and resurrection of Jesus Christ—real events that took place in a real place in the world more than two thousand years ago, a miracle of physical reality, spiritual transformation, and eternal consequence.

One way to explore these events is to examine the factual proofs of what happened. I could write about the physical evidence that Jesus really died and was not, as some have tried to argue, still alive when He was placed in the tomb. There is the evidence of the empty tomb itself and the circumstances that make it unlikely Jesus's body was stolen, as some have suggested. The resurrected Jesus appeared to many people over a period of time, verifying that He was very much physically alive after His death and burial. Volumes have been written about these things, and there is significant, specific historical evidence that the resurrection of Jesus actually and literally happened.

My friend Lee Strobel has written a powerful, best-selling book called *The Case for Christ* in which he tells about his extraordinary journey from being a

188 • Jesus: The Life Giver

hardened atheist to a committed Christ follower. Lee, an investigative journalist, spent a year examining the evidence for the resurrection of Christ. At the end of his research, he was faced with the overwhelming mountain of evidence that Christ truly rose from the dead.

After realizing that Christianity was not a blind leap of faith but, instead, a step of faith based on facts, Lee committed his life to Christ. If you are skeptical about the Resurrection or just have some questions, I highly recommend *The Case for Christ*.

A PERSONAL MIRACLE

What I want to focus on is not the overwhelming evidence of the Resurrection but something that overwhelms me when I read the gospel accounts of the Resurrection. I've read these Bible passages over and over, and this grabs my heart and won't let go.

The death and resurrection of Jesus are *immensely, specifically personal.*

This story is about people, about ordinary men and women like you and me. It is about Peter slicing off a soldier's ear to defend Jesus and then only hours later denying three times that he even knew the man. It is about the traitor Judas. It is about Joseph of Arimathea, who provided the tomb for Jesus's body. It is about the centurion at the foot of the cross. It is about Mary, Jesus's mother, whom Jesus addressed while nailed to the cross. It is about Pilate, the Roman ruler who didn't know what to do when the crowd demanded crucifixion for this innocent man. And then a few days later, it is about Thomas, who doubted, and Mary Magdalene, who mourned, and John "the disciple whom Jesus loved" (John 21:7).

In this grand epic, one that reveals the cosmic significance of Christ's death, the camera stays tight, comes in close, and focuses on the faces of ordinary people.

I'm sure this is no accident. The meaning of this miracle is cosmic indeed, but even more it is intimate. This miracle is about human hearts and the souls of men and women and how they respond to this jaw-dropping moment in time, this epic true story, this grand miracle. As transcendent as God is, He is also immanent, personal, up close.

He isn't just out there but in here.

In the faces of these individuals that we might think are just bit players, we see reflections of ourselves. Each person, in one way or another, had given up. Inside each of them was a miracle-need like those we experience today. And the way those individuals responded to that time-stopping moment as they looked into the eyes of Jesus might well reflect how we respond to Jesus today.

THE VEIL OF UNBELIEF

The Roman centurion who presided over the crucifixion had undoubtedly witnessed many criminals being executed for their crimes. He had probably played a part in brutally suppressing pockets of rebellion as the Roman Empire exercised its power to control the masses.

This Roman soldier was well acquainted with the harsh realities and injustices of life. Day after day of dealing with human misery and pain and the stark reality of sin and despair in his own life had perhaps caused him to give up on experiencing anything beyond the darkness.

I believe a veil of unbelief had settled over his heart and kept him from seeing beyond the painful present, a veil that kept him in a state of spiritual blindness and complete hopelessness.

Sometimes our painful present does create a veil over our spiritual eyes, and it keeps us from seeing beyond the harsh realities of life. Maybe you are a bit like the Roman centurion in that you've seen and experienced a lot of pain and sorrow, and you have almost given up hope that there is anything beyond the brokenness.

Maybe you, too, are having trouble seeing through the veil of the painful present to a hope-filled future.

The Roman soldier probably would not have known about an actual veil that was hanging not far from the crucifixion site. In the Jewish temple a heavy curtain called a veil separated the inner room, the Holy of Holies, from the rest of the temple. The veil was made of fine linen and was embroidered with blue, scarlet, and purple yarn.

The Roman soldier, who spoke only Latin, would not have known that the word for "veil" in Hebrew means "screen" and referred to a barrier that separates. He would not have known this veil separated a perfectly pure and holy God from the unholy presence of sinful people.

Although the Roman guard may have not known much about Jewish religious practice, he might have sensed in his life a distance and separation from the divine, true, living God. Perhaps this Roman had struggled with the myths of his people, the pantheon of gods that Romans followed and worshiped. Perhaps those gods seemed distant, cold, and dead. Perhaps the centurion knew those gods weren't real but the veil of unbelief made it hard for him to see that anything other than pain and suffering were real.

The Roman soldier looked up into the darkening sky. Above him loomed three crosses. This man Jesus hung in the middle. The centurion and his men guarded the crucifixion site, making sure that Pilate's sentence was carried out without interference from the Jewish mobs. Of all the crucifixions he had witnessed, he had never seen one quite like this.

He had heard about this man Jesus and the miracles He'd performed, the things He'd taught, the crowds who had followed Him. Who hadn't heard? This news had spread throughout the region. Everyone knew.

Perhaps the Roman centurion wondered who Jesus really was. After all, that was the whole point of the trials before Pilate and Herod. Jesus claimed to be God, the Jewish Pharisees claimed that was blasphemy, and that forced the trial, which resulted in the sentence of death. Perhaps the Roman was curious how Jesus could perform miracles in people's lives if he wasn't God.

Maybe this Roman centurion found himself looking up and thinking about the miracle he needed right there and then. *If only . . .*

We don't know. This story of the centurion at Jesus's crucifixion is short. Just a few verses. But he is an intriguing character because of what happened next.

It was the middle of the afternoon, but, strangely, the sky was dark. The centurion standing there heard Jesus cry out, "My God, my God, why have you forsaken me?" (Matthew 27:46). He saw Jesus's mother and some of His followers watching and grieving at this bloody, tragic scene. But others mocked Jesus, derisively calling out for Elijah to save Him. Someone ran to get a sponge soaked with wine and vinegar to deaden Jesus's pain. He took it and cried out, "It is finished" (John 19:30).

The Roman centurion then heard the final words of this man Jesus: "Father, into your hands I commit my spirit" (Luke 23:46).

Immediately there was an earthquake. The ground shook, rocks split, and "tombs broke open" (Matthew 27:52).

In the temple nearby, the veil—the curtain separating humanity from God—tore right down the middle (see Mark 15:38).

Precisely at that moment the centurion's veil was lifted from his eyes, and he exclaimed, "Surely this man was the Son of God!"

I believe in that moment this Roman centurion received the miracle he needed—the miracle of a real God reaching out to him and rescuing him from unbelief.

I also believe that you and I need this same miracle above all other miracles. This is the miracle of salvation—God rescuing us, pulling us out of our sin, redeeming us. This is the work of Jesus taking on our sins so the veil can be torn away and God can be present with us, not distant and separate. This is the miracle of eternal life with God, life that starts now and continues beyond time.

Again, I believe that the stories of the people who were at Jesus's crucifixion and resurrection are our stories as well. At one point of my life, I was like the centurion who stood guard at the foot of the cross. Perhaps you see yourself in him as well.

The miracle the centurion needed was knowledge of the real God. I believe a miracle happened there and then, and it involved tearing away the veil. The partition between God and humanity, and the veil of unbelief on this Roman's eyes—both veils were torn. When the centurion's tore, he saw and proclaimed that this Jesus was indeed the Son of God and that there was something beyond his present pain.

I wonder if you need this miracle today but you have a veil over your eyes. I wonder if you are facing storm clouds in your life and don't know the God who is real. I wonder what might happen if, against the backdrop of your day's darkness, you looked into the loving, saving eyes of Jesus, the Son of God, who died for you.

SCRIPT CHANGE

John Glenn was the first American to orbit the earth. Like many of the NASA astronauts, he found that being in space prompted big thoughts about God and faith. He said, "To look up out at this kind of creation and not believe in God is to me impossible. . . . It just strengthens my faith."[27] Other astronauts since then have echoed Glenn's statements. Buzz Aldrin observed the Lord's Supper while he was on the moon.[28]

But perhaps more famous is the quote attributed to Russian cosmonaut Yuri Gagarin, who was the first man to travel into space. He was quoted as saying, "I flew into space, but didn't see God," and this comment created a furor in the Cold War era between a "Christian" America and an atheistic Soviet Union.[29]

Some two thousand years earlier this may have been the dilemma one of Jesus's disciples faced. And maybe it's a struggle for you as well.

We call him "doubting Thomas," but I think that's a bad rap. In many ways

Thomas wrestled with questions we all have wrestled with, and he struggled to believe the astonishing events his fellow disciples had told him about.

There are only a few passages in the Bible that give us insight into the character of Thomas. One is the story of Lazarus. When Mary and Martha asked Jesus to come to Bethany to heal Lazarus, many of His disciples were wary of going there because they deemed it to be dangerous. We need to remember that Jesus and His disciples were regarded as revolutionaries, and many of the Jewish leaders opposed Jesus. As the disciples debated the wisdom of going to Bethany, it was Thomas who showed revolutionary zeal and said, "Let us also go, that we may die with him" (John 11:16).

I think it's possible that Thomas was a revolutionary following a man he considered a revolutionary leader. Maybe Thomas thought Jesus was the Messiah who would bring down the current government. At the time, that was a common assumption. Many who followed Jesus, including many of the disciples, thought the Messiah would be the rebel king and would lead Israel in overthrowing the evil Roman government and establishing a new kingdom.

But that was not Jesus's job description.

In another brief passage we see Thomas's response after one of Jesus's famous teachings. Jesus said, "Do not let your hearts be troubled. You believe in God; believe also in me. My Father's house has many rooms; if that were not so, would I have told you that I am going there to prepare a place for you? And if I go and prepare a place for you, I will come back and take you to be with me that you also may be where I am. You know the way to the place where I am going" (John 14:1–4).

Thomas, it seems, assumed Jesus was speaking about ascending to an earthly throne. He responded, "Lord, we don't know where you are going, so how can we know the way?" (verse 5).

Thomas wanted the facts. He was asking for a map to the new royal palace.

In the miracles of Jesus, you and I have seen over and over how many people wrestled with the core question "Who is Jesus?" It took His disciples a long time to figure it out. In fact, I believe some of them still hadn't figured it out when Jesus rose from the grave. Thomas, the revolutionary, was one who still wrestled with who Jesus was.

I think at times you and I haven't figured it out either. Like Thomas, we may approach Jesus expecting something different. We have a job description for Him, and we're disappointed if He doesn't fulfill it as we expect Him to. If He doesn't do this thing for us or doesn't save us from that problem, we may feel that Jesus isn't doing the miracle we want.

Like Thomas, we want Jesus to fit our image of who He is. And when he doesn't, we kind of give up. Thomas believed Jesus was the revolutionary Messiah—but something had gone terribly wrong. Now Jesus was dead.

As the Bible tells us, after His resurrection Jesus appeared to His disciples, but Thomas wasn't in the room that night. The disciples later told Thomas in breathless tones, "We have seen the Lord!"

Skeptical Thomas didn't know what to do with this information because it didn't fit his definition of Jesus. Jesus wasn't supposed to die. A Messiah doesn't do that. And then come back to life? What? That's not in the script either. No, Thomas had given up on Jesus because nothing had happened the way he thought it should.

I wonder if you and I sometimes find ourselves caught in moments of doubt because the real Jesus—who He really is—just doesn't fit our script for Him.

Thomas defiantly replied, "Unless I see the nail marks in his hands and put my finger where the nails were, and put my hand into his side, I will not believe it." He needed evidence of who Jesus really was.

The other thing that I think tripped up Thomas, and may trip us too, is a belief in the God up there but a lack of faith in the God right here.

Thomas could look into the heavens and see the handiwork of the God out there. Even though Thomas couldn't see the universe as vividly as astronauts have, the wonders of creation—the stars, the moon, the sun—were perhaps enough for him to believe in the God out there. But apparently he struggled to believe that Jesus could be the God right here.

Show me Your wounds, Thomas insisted, *because the last time I saw You, You were dead on a cross, and I have no category for a revolutionary who dies and then comes back from the dead.*

So Thomas was a doubter, but as I said, I think he gets a bad rap for that. I don't think doubt is a bad thing. I don't think it's a sin. I don't think it's incompatible with faith. In fact, I think doubt is a *requirement* of faith. That is, if you have no doubt, if you are perfectly *certain,* then you don't need faith.

I don't think the problem with Thomas was that he doubted but that he required certainty.

Jesus hinted at this with Thomas. He indulged Thomas's request for more data and showed His crucifixion wounds to him. When Thomas finally saw the wounded Jesus of the cross, Thomas believed, exclaiming, "My Lord and my God!"

Jesus replied, "Because you have seen me, you have believed; blessed are those who have not seen and yet have believed." Jesus was saying that Thomas had been given virtual certainty, but others would not have as much evidence. Those people who have faith without seeing all the facts will be blessed.

I think we all have our Thomas moments. We might question God because we were expecting something different from Him. The miracle we were seeking didn't happen, and we don't have a script for what did happen. Or we might go through times when we believe in the God out there, but we struggle to see the God right here with us. We might have doubts, as Thomas did, and we toss and turn in the midst of them.

I think this is part of the journey of faith.

As Thomas did, we find our miracle in the miracle of the Resurrection. In the Grand Miracle, we finally can put together the God of outer space with the

Jesus of inner space. Jesus enters into our presence and allows us to touch His wounds.

Even as He heals our own.

BARRIERS INTO BRIDGES

In 1907 a bridge was nearing completion in Canada. It spanned the St. Lawrence River and was needed to connect the north shore of Quebec City with the south shore across the river.

It was a massive and expensive project that required an Act of Parliament. Funds were allocated and construction began. By 1904 the southern portion of the bridge had been completed.

However, what wasn't known at the time was that some of the plans had never been properly checked. Calculations were off; disaster was imminent.

Construction continued.

On August 29, 1907, as workers neared quitting time, the central section of the Quebec Bridge collapsed into the river. Of eighty-six workers on the bridge that day, seventy-six were killed. It was a national tragedy. An investigation of the collapse concluded that the shoddy planning was the primary cause.

Not quite ten years later, work commenced on rebuilding the bridge. Incredibly, again there was a major disaster, and the central span of the bridge fell into the river as it was being hoisted up. Thirteen workers were killed.[30]

These tragic events illustrate that something can be broken before it breaks, that it is faulty before it collapses. I think this is so true of us in life. We are broken people to start with. Yet when our lives fall apart, we act surprised.

I think this was true of Peter, who walked with Jesus through His ministry on earth and through His trial and death. Peter went through so many ups and downs. How many times did he crash and burn?

Peter walked on water and then suddenly had that sinking feeling. At another time Jesus said to Peter, "Get behind me, Satan!" (Matthew 16:23). Ouch.

And the night before Jesus's death, Peter jumped to the defense of Jesus in the garden, cutting off the ear of the high priest's servant. Then hours later in the courtyard he denied that he even knew Jesus. In fact, he denied Jesus *three* times.

I think one of Peter's problems was that he tried too hard. And we do too. That is, we try to make our way to God. We strive to reach Him in some way, to build a bridge to God. Peter was earnest, urgent, and even reckless in building his bridge to get to Jesus.

All the other religions of the world are about this. They ask, "How do we reach God?" And those religions are based on the things we need to do or be in order to get to God. In essence, they are in the business of building a bridge to God.

But the great distinctive of the Christian faith is that we don't need to build a bridge to God. He has already built the bridge. And walked across it. God has come to us.

Religion says, "You better keep building." Religion tells you, "Don't give up on building a perfect life. Don't give up on building perfect relationships. Don't give up on building a bridge of good works that will take you to heaven."

Christianity, on the other hand, says that you can stop trying to build your weak, pathetic, and faulty bridge to heaven, because the real one is already built. It says stop trying to build a perfect life in your own power, because you're hopelessly broken.

So when you come to the place of giving up, you're on the verge of a miracle. We keep coming back to the part of the Miracle Map that says God works His miracles when we're at the end of our rope.

I spent my high school summers lifeguarding at the community pool. I'll never forget the long hours of certification training that started at six in the morning in a cold pool.

I'll also never forget Mrs. Simmons and how seriously she took the responsibility of training high school kids how to save a life.

One part of the training was that I had to swim into the deep end of the pool and save a drowning victim who was in a panicked frenzy—a role played by Mrs. Simmons. I quickly got out to her and tried to implement the life-saving techniques and take her safely to the side of the pool. But Mrs. Simmons should have won an Academy Award for playing someone in total panic just before going under. She was so strong that she pulled me under, and I remember thinking, *She has forgotten this is just a drill! I think I'm going to drown!* I finally struggled free and came up for a much needed gasp of air.

Mrs. Simmons's portrayal of a drowning victim seared into my mind the lesson she was trying to get across: *You can't save people until they stop trying to save themselves!*

I later learned that when you spot panicked swimmers, you swim out to them, but before you try to rescue them, you let them flail away until they wear themselves out and start to go under. Then you swim closer and rescue them. If you try to save them while they are still trying to save themselves, both of you might drown!

Similarly, God won't do His saving work in your life until you stop trying to save yourself. He waits until all your prideful flailing stops and you finally give up and start to go under. Then He works the miracle you need most.

The first great message of the Resurrection miracle is that God is here. He built the bridge.

The second message is that God is really good at restoring broken bridges and broken people.

Maybe you're looking into your future and all you can see is brokenness. Or maybe all you can see is a huge barrier, a huge problem, and you feel powerless to overcome it. Maybe you feel you can never change.

The miracle of the Resurrection is that God loves to take barriers and turn them into bridges. That's why I believe the greatest barrier in your life is really a bridge in disguise.

After Peter denied Jesus three times, it's likely he watched Jesus die. Who knows what anguish he felt deep within his soul, having tried so hard to do his best for Jesus, only to fail so miserably at a crucial moment. I'd bet he was in despair and shock. The bridge he had built was collapsing, and his own denials had helped bring it down. I believe Peter was at the place of giving up.

Does that feel familiar?

But then on the third day . . .

Yes, Jesus rose from the dead. Several times He appeared to His disciples, Peter included. But there was a moment when Jesus and Peter were on the shore of the Sea of Galilee, where so much of their life stories had played out together. And at this moment Jesus spoke to Peter in the most intimate way:

> When they had finished eating, Jesus said to Simon Peter, "Simon son of John, do you love me more than these?"
>
> "Yes, Lord," he said, "you know that I love you."
>
> Jesus said, "Feed my lambs."
>
> Again Jesus said, "Simon son of John, do you love me?"
>
> He answered, "Yes, Lord, you know that I love you."
>
> Jesus said, "Take care of my sheep."
>
> The third time he said to him, "Simon son of John, do you love me?"
>
> Peter was hurt because Jesus asked him the third time, "Do you love me?" He said, "Lord, you know all things; you know that I love you."
>
> Jesus said, "Feed my sheep." (John 21:15–17)

We don't know if Peter understood the deeper meaning of this conversation. That Jesus was entrusting His future church to Peter's care. That after all the crashing and burning of Peter's life, Jesus would talk to him in such a personal way and say, "I'm leaving these people I love to your care." But surely Peter could feel the trust Jesus had placed in him.

Bridge reconstructed. Peter restored. His future assured.

The third time Jesus asked Peter, "Do you love Me?" Scripture says that

Peter was hurt. I think he was probably hurt because it caused him to remember his greatest failure. He had denied Jesus three times, and he was asked three times by Jesus, "Do you love Me?"

I don't think Jesus was trying to hurt Peter or make him feel guilty about his sin that had already been forgiven. I do think, however, that Jesus wanted Peter always to remember how much he needed God's power. Sometimes the hurt we feel from past failures is a good thing because it drives us into the powerful and loving arms of the Healer.

Jesus wasn't condemning Peter. Jesus was calling him to fulfill his destiny to be the rock upon which He would build His church.

The miracle of the Resurrection is this: God can take your greatest mess and turn it into your greatest message of hope. God can take your greatest pain and use it to help you fulfill your greatest purpose in life. God can take your biggest barrier and turn it into the very bridge that takes you to your calling.

God loves to do that.

He has a way of turning crucifixions into resurrections.

THE THREE GARDENS

The miracle of the Resurrection is a story of three gardens.

The first is the Garden of Eden. It's the start of the whole story of God and humanity, the reason a miracle was needed. Originally Eden was for Adam and Eve the garden of fulfillment, the garden of purpose, the garden of life. Adam and Eve were created for relationship, for soul connection, with God and with each other. And this was the wonderland for this beautiful union. But we know the story. Satan tempted, Adam and Eve sinned, and the relationships were destroyed. I believe the Garden of Eden was a real place on earth. But I also believe it is a spiritual garden within each person's heart that needs to be restored.

The second garden in this cosmic story is the Garden of Gethsemane, the place where Jesus, the Son of God, prepared for His capture and death, prayed to God, and kept His disciples from messing up everything. "Then Jesus went with them to the olive grove called Gethsemane, and he said, 'Sit here while I go over there to pray.' . . . He told them, 'My soul is crushed with grief to the point of death. Stay here and keep watch with me'" (Matthew 26:36, 38, NLT).

On a visit to the Holy Land, I stood next to an ancient olive tree in the Garden of Gethsemane, one where Jesus Himself possibly knelt and prayed. Gethsemane was a garden of grief and anguish because of the extraordinary event that was about to take place. It was a dark, lonely place for Jesus as He experienced the immense weight of the coming hours, the realization that He was going to the cross to take on the iniquities of the world—the terrible atrocities of humankind and all the sins in my life and yours—that keep us from communion with a perfect God.

The third garden in the miracle of the Resurrection is referred to as the Garden Tomb, the area where Jesus's tomb was located. This was where the resurrected Jesus was first encountered by just one person who was unaware of the cosmic significance of this garden in relation to the first two.

It was a woman, and her name was Mary Magdalene.

The Bible says, "When Jesus rose early on the first day of the week, he appeared first to Mary Magdalene, out of whom he had driven seven demons" (Mark 16:9). Luke reported what had happened earlier with Mary:

Soon afterward [Jesus] went on through cities and villages, proclaiming and bringing the good news of the kingdom of God. And the twelve were with him, and also some women who had been healed of evil spirits and infirmities: Mary, called Magdalene, from whom seven demons had gone out, and Joanna, the wife of Chuza, Herod's household manager, and Susanna, and many others, who provided for them out of their means. (Luke 8:1–3, ESV)

Mary Magdalene had been healed by Jesus earlier in His ministry when He freed her of demons, and she became a Christ follower. In fact, she apparently became part of the entourage that helped support the ministry of Jesus and the disciples.

We don't hear much more about Mary Magdalene until these final chapters of Jesus's life on earth. She is present in the accounts of Jesus's death. She was one of the group that stayed close to the cross during Jesus's final hours. And she was the first one to appear at the tomb that Sunday morning of the Grand Miracle.

I think Mary Magdalene may have been someone much like you and me. Quite simply, are you someone who has followed Jesus for a long time? Someone who has served God in many ways for many months and years? And are you tired, weary, and perhaps a bit disillusioned in your faith?

Mary must have been heartbroken watching the Jesus she had followed and loved endure the agony of the cross. Who knows what she thought about who Jesus was—God or the Messiah or a revolutionary or a future king. She served her Lord—we know that. But I have to think that after Jesus died on the cross and His body was taken down and buried, her world was shaken. Perhaps she was thinking about going back to the ordinary world she had lived in before she encountered Jesus.

Is this you too? Has your encounter with Jesus become tired and faded? Have you lost your first passion for God? Do you feel yourself returning to the ordinary world you started in?

Is the miracle you need a fresh encounter with the living God?

Listen to the account of Mary's encounter with the resurrected Jesus. See yourself in it.

Mary was standing outside Jesus's tomb in the garden, one of the three biblical gardens that mark the cosmic story of God, humanity, and redemption. She was about to become a significant part of this epic event, but she didn't realize it.

She was crying. We might suppose her grief had blinded her to the circumstances there. The tomb was open, the stone had been rolled away, and two angels were there. The angels asked why she was crying.

She answered, "They have taken my Lord away." And her next statement is heartbreaking: "I don't know where they have put him."

You can hear the deep sorrow and complete hopelessness in her voice. She was at the place of giving up.

I think this is profound. You and I have at times drifted away from our Jesus, thinking He wasn't there and we didn't really know where He was. Of course, He was there. He is always there, but we don't know where.

Jesus was standing behind Mary. He called out to her, "Woman, why are you crying? Who is it you are looking for?"

Mary did not recognize Him. From other passages we know that Jesus's appearance after His resurrection was different. He had a body, but it was transcendent. And He had the ability to reveal His identity or not as He wished. It might also be that Mary couldn't see clearly because of the tears in her eyes. Sometimes it's hard to see Jesus when our eyes are filled with tears. Sometimes our sorrow keeps us from seeing clearly. When we've given up, we stop looking. God will never leave you or forsake you, but when you are hurting so badly, you may not feel His presence. But even when you can't feel His presence, He is there. In fact, when you're brokenhearted, Scripture says, He's closer than ever (see Psalm 34:18). It's just hard to see clearly through the tears. Mary couldn't see who Jesus truly was, and in one of the most beautiful dialogues in all of Scripture, she imagined Him to be the gardener.

She asked the "gardener" if he knew where Jesus was. She wanted to know because she would then get His body.

This case of mistaken identity is poignant, charming, and even funny. And it's also true. Jesus was One with God the Father at Creation, meaning He literally created the Garden of Eden. In His teachings on earth, He often told stories about vineyards and vines and figs and tending soil. When He stood outside the

Garden Tomb with Mary Magdalene, who believed Him to be the gardener, Jesus was the Gardener in some ways.

Then the moment happened. Jesus called her by her first name: "Mary." Jesus revealed His identity.

My question is this. In your current place of discouragement and despair, can you hear Jesus calling your name? Can you hear in His voice the same tone He used with Mary—compassion, joy, love? If so, what will you do? How will you respond?

Mary turned—we can only imagine her astonishment—and called Him "Teacher!" And she ran to Him. The Master Gardener.

Maybe you've been a Christian for a long time, maybe you've gone through spiritual ups and downs, and maybe your vineyard has grown dry. You need to find a miracle. That miracle is the risen Christ. It is the miracle of the Resurrection. Even though you've already given your life to Jesus, perhaps just like Mary Magdalene you despair over where they've put your Jesus. Or maybe you've just forgotten where *you've* put Him.

Let me suggest this to you: Turn around. Listen to Jesus speak your name. Go running to Him. And then, as Mary did, exclaim the good news, "I have seen the Lord!"

PERSONAL RESURRECTION

The resurrection of Jesus is a cosmic event with a personal impact.

In the lives of the Roman centurion, Thomas, Simon Peter, Mary Magdalene, and others, we see images of ourselves. Maybe they are reflections of us at different stages of life, or maybe they remind us of recurring situations in our lives. They were ordinary people like you and me. They were in need of a miracle, just as we are.

The death and resurrection of Jesus is an event that often is thought of as being for the unbeliever, perhaps like the Roman centurion. It is that, but it is more. It is also for the one who is close to belief and in some ways does believe but has some questions and doubts. Like Thomas, we need the miracle of assurance that Jesus brings to us; we need to touch His wounds. The death and resurrection of Jesus is also a miracle for those whose lives are marked by great ups and downs, as Peter's life was, with its soaring successes and depressing failures. And there is the moment of intimate reunion with Jesus looking into our eyes and saying "I trust you." The resurrection of Jesus is a miracle of His remarkable connection with you in a garden when He speaks your name, and you turn and run into His arms.

In all these ways the Resurrection is the personal miracle you've been seeking.

The degree and dimension of Jesus's sacrifice, the brilliance of God's grace in giving His Son to die for our sin, and the extraordinary triumph of Christ's resurrection make this the Grand Miracle.

Through this, Jesus overcame death. Through this, Jesus conquered evil. Through this, Jesus transformed life for all eternity.

Christ is risen!

He is risen indeed!

Promises for When You've Given Up

He will wipe every tear from their eyes. There will be no more death or mourning or crying or pain, for the old order of things has passed away.

Revelation 21:4

Why, my soul, are you downcast?
Why so disturbed within me?
Put your hope in God,
for I will yet praise him,
my Savior and my God.

Psalm 42:5

LORD, sustain me as you promised, that I may live!
Do not let my hope be crushed.

Psalm 119:116, NLT

I pray that God, the source of hope, will fill you completely with joy and peace because you trust in him. Then you will overflow with confident hope through the power of the Holy Spirit.

Romans 15:13, NLT

What a God we have! And how fortunate we are to have him, this Father of our Master Jesus! Because Jesus was raised from the dead, we've been given a brand-new life and have everything to live for, including a future in heaven—and the future starts now!

God is keeping careful watch over us and the future. The Day is coming when you'll have it all—life healed and whole.

1 Peter 1:3–5, MSG

The LORD will fight for you; you need only to be still.

Exodus 14:14

The LORD is close to the brokenhearted;
    he rescues those whose spirits are crushed.

Psalm 34:18, NLT

For it is by grace you have been saved, through faith—and this is not from yourselves, it is the gift of God—not by works, so that no one can boast.

Ephesians 2:8–9

12

When You're Longing for New

Jesus Turns Water into Wine

The next day there was a wedding celebration in the village of Cana in Galilee. Jesus' mother was there, and Jesus and his disciples were also invited to the celebration. The wine supply ran out during the festivities, so Jesus' mother told him, "They have no more wine."

"Dear woman, that's not our problem," Jesus replied. "My time has not yet come."

But his mother told the servants, "Do whatever he tells you."

Standing nearby were six stone water jars, used for Jewish ceremonial washing. Each could hold twenty to thirty gallons. Jesus told the servants, "Fill the jars with water." When the jars had been filled, he said, "Now dip some out, and take it to the master of ceremonies." So the servants followed his instructions.

When the master of ceremonies tasted the water that was now wine, not knowing where it had come from (though, of course, the servants knew), he called the bridegroom over. "A host always serves the best wine first," he said. "Then, when everyone has had a lot to drink, he brings out the less expensive wine. But you have kept the best until now!"

This miraculous sign at Cana in Galilee was the first time Jesus revealed his glory.

—John 2:1–11, NLT

AFTER EXPLORING THE GRANDEST MIRACLE of all, there's a reason we conclude by looking briefly at the very first miracle Jesus performed.

And that very first miracle is also the most puzzling.

At the wedding in Cana, Jesus turned the water that filled huge jars into a reservoir of fine wine for a wedding reception. It was not a question of whether He could do it. Of course He could—and did. But this miracle is puzzling because it seems so different from all the miracles that follow.

Most of Jesus's miracles involved a specific person. Most miracles met a deep need of someone who was diseased or dying, impoverished, cast away by society, or underprivileged. And many of the miracles, as we have seen, offered provision, sustenance, rescue, and even life after death.

This one feels different. The miracle at the wedding at Cana wasn't directed toward a specific person, wasn't helping the downtrodden, and didn't meet a deep need—unless you think that running out of wine at a posh wedding reception is a terrible crisis.

It seems the miracles of Jesus shouldn't be about giving luxuries to well-off people. A "Jesus miracle" shouldn't be a parlor trick on a sunny afternoon at a society gathering. It shouldn't be a cute little bit of magic that elicits applause from the host and the guests.

So what *is* this about?

We need to remember this Miracle Map principle: *God's miracle in your life will always bring glory to Himself and point people to Jesus.* God has a purpose in everything. In some way this miracle must be saying something about that purpose, about Jesus Christ, and about you and me.

THE BEST FOR LAST

There's a bit of light comedy in this story, don't you think?

Jesus and His mother were at this wedding reception. The catering company had a problem—they ran out of Cabernet. And the reception had barely started. All they could serve was water.

Mary came to her Son's side and whispered, "There's a problem."

Now this sounds just like a mother and son at a wedding. Mom, close to the wedding hosts and perhaps the bride and groom (as some scholars suggest), learned of the wine shortage and sidled up to her son. She explained the situation to Jesus, and the clear implication was "Son, You need to do something."

Jesus replied, "Dear woman, that's not our problem." I believe this speaks to the puzzlement we have regarding this miracle: Jesus was saying that His ministry was not about supplying fine wine for wedding receptions. He added, "My time has not yet come," clearly meaning "God has a timetable for the next three years, and we don't want to get ahead of ourselves here."

Yet even after uttering those cautions, Jesus proceeded to work the miracle.

It's fun that we are offered a brief glimpse of the mother-Son relationship between Mary and Jesus. You almost see her flashing a knowing smile toward her Son as she turned to the caterers and said, "Do whatever he tells you." Mary knew who Jesus was, she knew what He could do, and she assumed that He would. It would make for a heart-warming story to think that Mary persuaded her Son Jesus to come to the rescue of the wedding hosts.

Yet we know differently. Mary did not in any way compel Jesus to do a miracle that God wasn't already going to do. We know that even in the light-hearted fun of this celebration time God had purposes that transcended saving the reputation of the wedding hosts—purposes that, in fact, transcend time itself.

Jesus started to give instructions.

Huge clay jars were filled with water. Liquid was ladled out for the master of ceremonies to taste. He drank. It was wine. And not wine stretched with water, but rich, full-bodied wine. Good wine. It was so good, in fact, that the emcee commended the host: "You've saved the best for last."

The master of ceremonies could not know that those words applied to Jesus Christ Himself. He could not know that this wine would become a symbol of Jesus's blood. He could not know that changing water into wine was a symbol that foreshadowed the Living Water becoming the redeeming blood of God's Son on the cross.

You see, this miracle at the very beginning of Jesus's ministry pointed to the ongoing miracle Christ works in people today.

This miracle was nothing less than a miracle of transformation, a beautiful symbol of how God can change ordinary people into something completely new, rich, full, and glorious.

How He creates new lives from old jars.

New Lives

An astonishing number of people have left their old lives behind. At some point they literally walked away from their homes, jobs, families, friends, and other relationships in order to start new lives, incognito, somewhere else.

Many of these people found themselves in financial trouble, scrapes with the law, or troubled relationships, so they escaped their old lives and created anonymous new lives. But some weren't running from the law; they were just fleeing dead lives. They tried to leave their old lives behind and start new lives somewhere else because they felt hopeless and miserable. In fact, I was surprised to learn there are articles online that offer advice and instruction on precisely how to walk away from one life in order to start another one.

I have to wonder about this. How can people walk away from family and friends so easily? I would say it surprises me, and yet it doesn't. I know that some people feel they are at the end of their rope, and chucking it all and starting a new life somewhere else is an attractive option. To them the fresh start offers freedom from debt, broken relationships, failed marriages, and bad job situations.

I shake my head at that kind of thinking, but then it occurs to me that as we look for a miracle, seeking a new life does have some appeal. Getting away from the old life and starting a new life is tempting. In a way, isn't that what our desire for a miracle is about? Don't we want to escape current circumstances? Don't we want to be free of our current health issues, financial issues, and relationship issues? Don't we reach out for a miracle in hopes of finding a new and better life?

The truth is, we all want to leave some aspects of our old lives behind and start brand-new lives without the mess.

The problem is, you can't get away from *yourself.* Wherever you go, whatever you try to start new, *you're* still there. That same person who got into the current mess is fully capable, even likely, to get into the same sort of messes again in a new life. The same soul who gets into the worst predicaments, relentless addictions, and ugliest relationships is simply going to take all that baggage to the new location.

If only there were a way for a person to be completely, utterly transformed.

Jesus's miracle of turning water into wine is a picture of the miracle He can do in you—and that is the utter transformation of the heart, a true change of the old into the new, and the promise of a life made new by redeeming the old. God takes the empty jars of your life, fills them with ordinary water, and—through the grand miracle of Jesus Christ Himself—turns that water into the finest, richest, most wonderful wine.

It's easy to physically leave where you are to make a fresh start, but a fresh start on the outside never changes anything. It's a fresh start on the inside—really from the inside out—that changes you and many times the people and the circumstances around you. That kind of new life is called redemption, the ongoing miracle God provides to us through Jesus Christ.

Yes, Jesus's earliest miracle is also His very latest. It's a miracle He performs fresh every day in the lives of ordinary people like you and me.

Here's the great news. No matter what has happened in your life up to this point, the Miracle Maker who turned water into wine and saved the best for last at the wedding of Cana has saved the best for last in your life. So follow the Source of miracles down the road of life, and the rest of your life can be the best of your life as you live in the miracle of His redeeming love.

Promises for a New Beginning

I will give you a new heart and put a new spirit in you; I will remove from you your heart of stone and give you a heart of flesh.

Ezekiel 36:26

Therefore, if anyone is in Christ, the new creation has come: The old has gone, the new is here!

2 Corinthians 5:17

Throw off your old sinful nature and your former way of life, which is corrupted by lust and deception. Instead, let the Spirit renew your thoughts and attitudes. Put on your new nature, created to be like God—truly righteous and holy.

Ephesians 4:22–24, NLT

"He will wipe every tear from their eyes, and there will be no more death or sorrow or crying or pain. All these things are gone forever."

And the one sitting on the throne said, "Look, I am making everything new!" And then he said to me, "Write this down, for what I tell you is trustworthy and true."

Revelation 21:4–5, NLT

See, I will create
    new heavens and a new earth.
The former things will not be remembered,
    nor will they come to mind.

Isaiah 65:17

Discussion Questions

1. The Miracle You Need Most
   - What miracles have you personally experienced or witnessed in the lives of others?
   - Describe some of the dangers you see in those who see miracles in everything that happens. What are the dangers of not believing in miracles at all?
   - What is the miracle you need most in this season of your life?

2. The Map to Your Miracle
   - The claim is made, "God always meets you at the point of your need." What does that mean to you?
   - Describe a miracle you experienced or heard about and how it led someone to a closer relationship to God.
   - One of the Miracle Map principles is that "God works the miracle in His time and in His way." Is this just an excuse for those miracles that don't seem to happen when we ask for them? Why or why not?

3. Positioning Yourself for a Miracle
   - What does it mean to position yourself to receive a miracle?
   - What might need to change in your own heart posture in order to prepare yourself to receive a miracle?
   - What is the difference between doing things to earn a miracle and preparing your heart to receive a miracle?

4. When You're Stuck

- What are some other instances in the Bible where water was significant in a story or event?
- What are some ways that you or others you know might be paralyzed in life?
- Talk about a miracle in your life or the lives of others that was totally unexpected.

5. When You're Desperate

- Share with others a time or two when you felt truly desperate.
- The chapter speaks of physical, emotional, relational, and spiritual healing. Without going into specifics, share with others which of those four is the miracle you need right now. As a group, pray for those needs, asking God to bring a miracle into each person's life.
- We don't think of the woman at the well as a miracle story. But was it? Explain why you answered as you did.

6. When You're Overwhelmed

- Spend a few minutes in silence remembering what God has done in your past. Then share with others some of those things.
- What is the BHAG—Big Hairy Audacious Goal—you find yourself facing right now? Why does it feel overwhelming to you?
- What is the "ripple effect"? When have you experienced it? Share one or two with the group.

7. When You're Discouraged

- Name something in your life—at home, at work, in a relationship—that has discouraged you lately. Which of the biblical promises at the end of the chapter gives you the most encouragement in your situation?

- What aspects of Peter's personality do you see in yourself? In what way(s)?
- What do you think you need to do to prepare yourself—to position yourself—to receive a miracle from God to fill those nets?

8. When You're Afraid

- Describe a storm in your life, past or present, that rose up suddenly.
- What is your understanding of the biblical phrase "the fear of the Lord"?
- Describe an occasion when, in a period of waiting, you felt God was asleep on the job. What ultimately happened in that situation?

9. When You're Lonely

- Sometimes adversities—the storms of life—have the effect of drawing us into ourselves, isolating us from others. When has this been true in your life? What effect did the isolation have on you?
- Describe a time in your life when you felt absolutely, utterly alone. What caused that feeling at some point to change?
- In practical terms what does it mean for you to focus your eyes on Jesus in your daily life?

10. When You're Hurting

- What experiences of facing death and being raised up again have you heard about?
- When, if ever, have you been angry at God? How did you express your anger?
- From the perspective of God's kingdom, what is the meaning of death? What is the meaning of life?

11. When You've Given Up

- What makes the birth, life, death, and resurrection of Jesus so "grand," as C. S. Lewis asserts?
- Think about the centurion, Thomas, Peter, and Mary Magdalene and where they were spiritually in the scenes mentioned. To which person do you most relate? Why?
- The statement is made that the resurrection of Jesus is a cosmic event with a personal impact. What does it mean that the Resurrection is a "cosmic event"? And what personal impact has it had on you?

12. When You're Longing for New

- Have you ever known anyone who has left behind his or her old life and started a new one elsewhere? What was the result?
- We often understand Christ's work on the cross as being about salvation, and it certainly is that. But how might we understand the Cross as an ongoing work of redemption in our daily lives? Explain.
- In what ways might God be working a miracle in your life today and changing you from within?

Acknowledgments

Thank you to Woodlands Church for your willingness to believe God for the impossible and for the way you inspire us with your faith.

Thank you to our unbelievably talented and dedicated staff at Woodlands Church, led by the incomparable Randy Reeves. A special thanks to Orla Mathwig for all your hard work and professionalism in helping us put the book together.

A heartfelt thank-you to all the talented team and dear friends at Water-Brook Multnomah, especially Alex Field and John Blase, for your tireless work on this project. You guys are miracle workers!

Thank you, Tom Winters. We love you.

Thank you, Ken Petersen, for working with us again to make this book all that we believe God wanted it to be. You are a true friend.

Thank you, Carol Bartley, for once again adding your invaluable touch to the process. You're the best!

Finally, we especially want to thank our fathers for their influence on this book. A lifetime of thanks to Dr. Damon Shook, whose powerful sermons have inspired so much of this book. We give our deepest gratitude to David Nelson for being an example of faith that inspires our faith beyond measure.

Notes

1. Bart D. Ehrman, *Jesus, Interrupted: Revealing the Hidden Contradictions in the Bible (and Why We Don't Know About Them)* (New York: HarperCollins, 2009), 173.
2. John Shelby Spong, "The Twelve Theses. A Call to a New Reformation," Koinonia, http://servicioskoinonia.org/relat/436e.htm.
3. "The Mighty Deeds of Jesus," Beliefnet, April 1, 2004, www.beliefnet .com/Faiths/Christianity/2004/04/The-Mighty-Deeds-Of-Jesus.aspx #TTzcZRQ33AmBPub3.99.
4. "Religion Among the Millennials," Pew Research Center, February 17, 2010, www.pewforum.org/2010/02/17/religion-among-the-millennials/.
5. C. S. Lewis, *Miracles*, Kindle edition (San Francisco: HarperCollins, 2001), 130.
6. Tiffany Youngblood Gilliam, "Everyday Miracles" in "12 Absolutely Amazing Miracles," Beliefnet, April 4, 2013, www.beliefnet.com/Faiths /Galleries/12-Absolutely-Amazing-Miracles. aspx?p=5#EBqOIioJ7ShHckKg.99.
7. Mark Batterson, *The Grave Robber: How Jesus Can Make Your Impossible Possible* (Grand Rapids: Baker Books, 2014), 14.
8. Lindsay Williams, "Unexpected Miracles: Natalie Grant's Story," Lifeway, May 4, 2016, www.lifeway.com/Article/unexpected-miracles-natalie -grant-bernie-herms-hurricane.
9. John 6:1–13.
10. Ray Stedman, "Do You Want to Get Well?" www.raystedman.org /new-testament/john/do-you-want-to-get-well.

11. "Just Drop the Blanket: The Moment You Never Noticed in *A Charlie Brown Christmas*," Crosswalk, December 14, 2015, www.crosswalk .com/special-coverage/christmas-and-advent/just-drop-the-blanket-the -moment-you-never-noticed-in-a-charlie-brown-christmas.html.

12. C. S. Lewis, *The Weight of Glory* (San Francisco: HarperCollins, 2001), 27.

13. Quoted in Ruth Bell Graham, *Prodigals and Those Who Love Them: Words of Encouragement for Those Who Wait* (Grand Rapids: Baker Books, 1999), 136.

14. "100,000 Stories to Prove Miracles Are for Real," Facebook, 2016, www .facebook.com/permalink.php?story_fbid=771354002935082&id=3973 29730337513.

15. Chris Shook and Megan Shook Alpha, *Beauty Begins: Making Peace with Your Reflection* (Colorado Springs, CO: WaterBrook, 2016), 59–61.

16. John F. Kennedy, Address to Congress on Urgent National Needs, May 25, 1961, "NASA Moon Landing," John F. Kennedy Presidential Library and Museum, www.jfklibrary.org/JFK/JFK-Legacy/NASA-Moon -Landing.aspx.

17. Quoted in James C. Collins and Jerry I. Porras, *Built to Last: Successful Habits of Visionary Companies* (New York: HarperCollins, 2004), 93.

18. John 2:1–11.

19. Belinda Burkitt, "Through Hard Times, a Family Finds Strength in Faith," MPR News, February 11, 2010, www.mprnews.org/story/2010 /02/11/burkitt.

20. Belinda Burkitt, "After 22 Months of Unemployment, a Small Miracle: A Job," MPR News, March 1. 2011, www.mprnews.org/story/2011/03/01 /burkitt.

21. Rick Weinberg, "94: Derek and Dad Finish Olympic 400 Together," ESPN, June 3, 2004, http://espn.go.com/espn/espn25/story?page =moments/94.

22. C. H. Spurgeon, *Morning and Evening* (London: Marshall Pickering, 1990), November 12.

23. McKenzie Romero, "Voice Heard by Baby Lily's Rescuers Came from Her Mother's Love, Family Says," *Deseret News,* March 16, 2015, www.deseretnews.com/article/865624403/Voice-heard-by-Baby-Lilys-rescuers-came-from-her-mothers-love-family-says.html?pg=all.

24. Ken Hulme, "Return from Death's Door: How God Brought Connie Davis Back to Life," CBN, www1.cbn.com/700club/return-deaths-door-how-god-brought-connie-davis-back-life.

25. C. S. Lewis, *The Grand Miracle* (New York: Ballantine, 1983), 55.

26. Lewis, *The Grand Miracle,* 55.

27. Seth Borenstein, "Astronauts' Faith Isn't Lost in Space," *Orlando Sentinel,* November 7, 1998, http://articles.orlandosentinel.com/1998-11-07/lifestyle/9811060642_1_astronauts-john-glenn-faith.

28. Buzz Aldrin, "Guideposts Classics: Buzz Aldrin on Communion in Space," Guideposts, www.guideposts.org/faith/stories-of-faith/guideposts-classics-buzz-aldrin-on-communion-in-space?nopaging=1.

29. Valentin Petrov, "Did Yuri Gagarin Say He Didn't See God in Space?" *Pravmir,* April 12, 2013, www.pravmir.com/did-yuri-gagarin-say-he-didnt-see-god-in-space/. It was later revealed that Gagarin never actually said this. The Soviet leader Nikita Khrushchev was the one who said it, but it was famously attributed to Gagarin. In fact, it was later discovered that Yuri Gagarin was actually a believer in Jesus Christ.

30. Robert Lewis with Rob Wilkins, *The Church of Irresistible Influence: Bridge-Building Stories to Help Reach Your Community* (Grand Rapids: Zondervan, 2002), 156.

Continue your personal journey with Kerry and Chris Shook

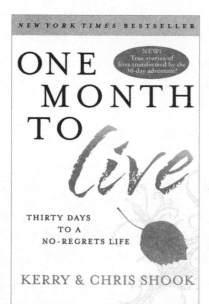

Discover the thirty-day process of learning to live passionately, love completely, learn humbly, and leave boldly. Make the most of your time on earth and live with no regrets.

Also Available:
• *One Month to Live Devotional Journal*
• *One Month to Live Guidebook*

Your relationships can go beyond Facebook and love-at-first-sight façades. Take the 30-Day Challenge for the adventure of a lifetime.

Previously released as *Love at Last Sight.*

Read an excerpt from these books and more at
www.WaterBrookMultnomah.com.

Your Life Is the Message

Living out the gospel in the world today is both simple and costly. Kerry and Chris Shook explore that paradox through biblical stories and their own experience of making a decision to live out the gospel in practical ways. Choosing to be the gospel changed their family, church, and personal relationship with God. How might it transform you?

**Read an excerpt from this book
and more at WaterBrookMultnomah.com**